BRUTE FORCE AND IGNORANCE

BRUTE FORCE AND IGNORANCE

Career Transition the Hard Way

ZACH MIERVA

Brute Force and Ignorance: Career Transition the Hard Way

© 2023 Zach Mierva

All rights reserved. No portion of this book may be reproduced, stored in a retrieval system, or transmitted in any form or by any means—electronic, mechanical, photocopy, recording, scanning, or other—except for brief quotations in critical reviews or articles, without the prior written permission of the author.

ISBN: 9798988237808

To My Family
You made me who I am today
You inspire me to be better
I love you with all my heart

CONTENTS

Preface	1
Introduction	7
Post 1: The Beginning, but Not the Start	19
Post 2: New Year, Better Me	25
Post 3: Prep Work	33
Post 4: Piling On	43
Post 5: Inspiration and Motivation	47
Post 6: Put in the Work	52
Post 7: Starting to Feel Real	63
Post 8: Career Highlights	69
Post 9: Culminating Event	75
Post 10: Recharge the Batteries	85
Post 11: Asking for Help	89
Post 12: The First Try	95
Post 13: Leading with Purpose	101
Post 14: Follow Through	108
Post 15: Networking, Redesigned	114
Post 16: Learning and Teaching	125
Post 17: You Can't be Weak	131
Post 18: One More Month	138
Post 19: The Final Class	147
Post 20: Small Steps Forward	153
Post 21: Not Goodbye, See You Soon	159

Post 22: Rear View Mirror	167
Post 23: 1,502 Miles	170
Post 24: New House, New Life	177
Post 25: Moving Nightmare	180
Post 26: Coming Together Nicely	182
Post 27: Accepting an Offer!	188
Post 28: If I Could Start Over	196
Conclusion	213
Gratitude and Acknowledgements	215
Appendix 1: Executive Checklist	218
Appendix 2: Consolidated List of Resources	220

PREFACE

I stared up at the massive mountain that is transitioning out of the service and into the private sector. I felt like I was about to embark on a climbing journey with the wrong equipment, and the metaphorical backpack I was carrying was the weight of supporting my family.

Something that has always been important to me is sharing lessons learned. I'm not sure where this mindset started, but I've found it to be a powerful tool to cement learning in myself and aid others in getting better. My friend Matt Rosebaugh did something similar a few years earlier, and after speaking with him I found myself motivated to provide something from my lens.

I was at a weird stage for "typical" military officer career transition: older than the average junior officer (who often pursues a Top-20 MBA and jumps into a killer job with rapid upward mobility), but not old enough to retire and have decades of experience to serve in higher-level corporate roles. It almost felt like living in a weird gray area where I had pigeon-holed myself, but I knew there was somewhere for me to go and to provide value and pursue my passions.

With my background in military leadership, my degree, and my desire to improve people and organizations, I was drawn to organizational development in some capacity. At the time I started my public reflection journal, I was focused on the Dallas area and leveraging United States Military Academy (USMA) Association of Graduates (AOG) Careers team, LinkedIn to network with USMA graduates, cold-contacting HR personnel in large companies, and applying to the Hiring Our Heroes program. For context, the USMA AOG Careers team helps graduates through the career transition process with helpful resources and coaching. I'll go into additional detail about their programs in the following sections.

It's also worth providing additional info about Hiring Our Heroes (HOH), another incredible group that helps veterans during career transition, as they offer a unique method within the Career Skills Program (CSP). The CSP is a government initiative, but the short version of that program is that it offers transitioning service members to essentially "intern" at companies, with the goal that the service member gains key job skills and experience, and hopefully gets hired by that company afterwards! HOH creates cohorts and has service members interview with prospective companies, then allows the service member and company to rank their top choices. Then HOH matches the two together and facilitates the CSP with weekly reflections. CSP is a great program that continues to improve, and HOH is an incredible resource that helps folks who might be struggling to find a "best fit" for an organization.

Let's get back to it. At that point, I had had some amazing conversations with some incredibly helpful people, and I took notes from our conversations to read over to save and leverage to ask better questions for the next meeting(s).

At the advice of Scott Leishman, who was part of the USMA AOG Careers team (and a family friend), I read *Designing Your Life*, and many of the lessons learned from doing the exercises in that book helped me refine my original ideas of "what I want to do when I grow up" into a better understanding of myself and my priorities. I also read *Atomic Habits*, which triggered me to leverage my own goal setting material that I teach to my students on myself to get one percent better every day. The public journaling was an attempt to force myself to stay committed.

The original idea was to be very informal and to adapt based on necessary changes, updates, and any feedback that I received. The format I used throughout the process was roughly built around a five-step concept:

1. Review what I did that week. I wanted this to serve as a recap for me to digest what I experienced, as well as provide a narrative to my audience to allow them to see the path I was walking.

2. Talk about my personal development. This was largely framed around what I was reading and learning. Some of the most impactful lessons I gleaned came from books, so this served as my way to share the most salient points.

3. Share a self-reflection of the week. I believe in demonstrating vulnerability to harness strength, and this served as an opportunity to show my scars. At times, it felt like everyone else had things figured out while they transitioned, and I wanted to show that wasn't the truth for everyone.

4. Share and reflect on my goal(s) progression. One of my biggest challenges is to stick to my goals, and I found that with an accountability partner (or in my case a public forum with thousands of eyeballs reading) I'm much more successful. Well, not just me—that's a human behavior thing. But I'm pretty bad at it, so I needed a method to keep me on track.

5. Express gratitude. No person is an island, and you don't get to where you're going without some assistance along the way. I also feel that one of the most powerful things you can do as a leader is to demonstrate your gratitude. My way was through this public forum to highlight the people who assisted me every week.

Out of simplicity, I thought about just copy-and-pasting my original posts into a Word document and trying to get someone to buy it. As much as that would be easier for me, I think it's lazy and frankly, you expect more out of me. Or you don't. (I really don't know you. I mean I might, but you know what I'm saying.) Then I remembered what I used to put on the back of my computer

PREFACE

monitor during tough times. LTC(R) Gus Grissom said: "Do good work." Or a way that was phrased to me in my military career: "Don't suck; it makes everyone else's job harder."

Let me rephrase how I'm going to approach this book: I'm going to do it the same way I did it before. Didn't see that coming, did you? One of my mentors, Rob Campbell, said, "Don't write the book for the audience; write it for yourself and the audience will find you." It wasn't until a few months later that I realized what this meant to me, and it aligns perfectly with why I started this process. I want to show the journey, my personal growth, and my gratitude to those who helped me find my next career. I found a treasure trove of resources to support transitioning service members, but not all are exclusive to those who served.

As an aside, the middle of this book may feel a bit disjointed. That's by design. I wrote 28 articles, one week at a time, and I believe it's valuable for you to see what that journey looked and felt like in real-time. I have synthesized much of the learning to share in other methods and captured a more focused look into who I am in the introduction and conclusion of this book. Those feel more personal and give you a peek into my mind. The articles were more focused on an external audience, even though I deliberately used them to reflect on my personal journey.

To help you reflect, I'm going to pose questions at the end of each entry to help you answer the question of "Who am I?" in a thoughtful way. They are designed with intentionality in mind to get your brain to work through some difficult things to trigger growth and development. As I tried to figure out who I was, I found myself fighting against a competing force. I suffer from imposter syndrome, and at times it can be pretty difficult to cope with. However, I know I'm not alone or unique. At the conclusion of each chapter, I will bring attention to the thoughts I experienced during that particular stage of my transition. Imposter syndrome manifests differently for each person and it was a constant source of anxiety throughout my entire transition journey, and I suspect it might be for you, too. I hope that seeing the thoughts in someone else's head is useful.

I also leveraged my professional, educational, and…well…a little *Brute Force and Ignorance,* to create exercises that are built to move the reader from where you are to taking "The Leap of Courage Across the Fear Gap." My greatest hope is that if you see how one person broke down the steps, made mistakes and successes, and shared their journey you too can find your way.

I figure with a dozen years of training people, a background in organizational psychology, and a career in leadership development I can take a crack at helping you out. I hope that by leveraging these prompts and exercises, you'll be able to open the door instead of ramming your head against the wall until it falls over (like I did).

The process worked for me, and I bet it will for you, too.

What do you say we get into it?

Introduction
MY LIFE IN A FEW PAGES, BECAUSE WHY NOT?

Oh, hi. I didn't see you there. Nice to meet you. I'm Zach, and you are? Do you come here often?

Okay, yeah, enough of that. Let's get down to business. Who am I and why should you care?

After being in uniform in some capacity for more than 15 years, I left the army in 2021. I went on a very calculated journey during my transition that went about 34% according to plan, so I figured why not share my path to hopefully increase your success rate?

Before we hop into the meat and potatoes, it might be helpful for you to understand a bit more about me and how I got here. Like, why did I leave the army? Don't get me wrong. I loved my job, I loved serving, and I loved the people I worked with. I was excited to move on to the next steps of my career and tackle the challenges that lay ahead.

Let's rewind a bit.

I was born and raised in Alaska. This is only relevant to my story because my family and the people around me raised me to serve. Not necessarily in the military, but there's this weird mindset of togetherness in Alaska that is difficult to explain without having lived there for an extended period. I grew up in a small town that had as many bars as churches and as many "hippies" as lifted "mudding" trucks. But we were all in things together against the wilderness.

Again, don't get me wrong, I didn't live out in the bush like some of those wild Discovery Channel shows, but that didn't change the community mindset. The best example I can think of is that at one point, there was a law that you literally could not drive past someone broke down on the side of the road without stopping to check up on them. This speaks to the idea that no matter who someone is, you help them. That stuck with me and still does to this day.

I also had an incredibly supportive and loving family who dealt with my shenanigans, even when I went down a strange path and grew out my hair at my "first try" at college before I enlisted. That was a weird time…oh, and I shaved it into a mullet with lightning bolts in the side…yeah, weird time. Oh! And I did that right before I got my first military ID. My drill sergeants laughed until they cried, and I did push-ups until I cried…

I don't mean to gloss over my background, but I'd rather save the biography to be written by somebody else (read: won't ever happen). Let's skip ahead.

I was failing pretty hard at my first try at college. I had applied to West Point out of high school, but never put forth the effort and was not selected. Or to put that a different way: I didn't deserve to attend a prestigious college. I needed to figure myself out. And lose, like, 60 pounds. So off I went to my "safety school," the University of Alaska-Fairbanks. It is a great school, but I yet again failed to apply myself to anything except drinking beer and figuring out how to minimize attending class.

Something needed to change.

And it did…after a 23-day bender. Hungover, I ended up at a recruiting station and enlisted as a medic in the Reserves. Side note: I didn't know if I was in the Reserves or the National Guard, that's how much of an idiot I was at that time. But I did make one good decision: get some discipline in my life.

I shipped off to basic training (after watching *Full Metal Jacket*, which I don't recommend doing if you don't want to scare the crap out of yourself) in August of 2005, and my life drastically changed. I found structure, discipline, and a passion for being a soldier. I met some wonderful, and truly unique people (this was in the "go-to-the-Army-or-go-to-jail" time and that allowed me to meet some interesting folks).

After basic I went to learn to be a medic in San Antonio and found a love for medicine. I would later go on the pre-med track at West Point, only to have my advisor bring me in and say that he wouldn't even send me to the pre-boards to go to the boards to try to get admitted, so I should find another major. Not the first, nor the last, of many punches to my ego.

Back to the story.

I finished up my training and absolutely loved being a medic, and while I was going through my initial training, I applied to West

Point again. I had done a...lackluster...application while in college and was deservedly denied admission a second time. I returned back to Alaska to figure out my next steps, and the opportunity came to go to Iraq to serve with a unit as a line medic. I volunteered (I didn't have a family like most of my unit, and I was ready to prove myself), and started doing all the fun pre-deployment preparations like writing your will and taking your "death photo." If you're wondering if the gravity of my profession ever hit me in a mature way, no. No, it did not until much later because I'm a giant man-child at heart.

As I finalized my prep and got ready to head to Colorado for additional training, seven days before my flight, I received a very interesting phone call.

"Is this Zach?"

"Yes..."

"Hi this is Senator Ted Stevens. Congratulations, you've been accepted into West Point!"

"Uh...I'm supposed to fly to Iraq next week."

"Well, you'd better figure that out. Good luck!"

Rest in peace, Uncle Ted. But the third time's a charm, right?

After much deliberation and some beers on the porch with my stepdad, Rob, I was coaxed into going to West Point instead of Iraq. If it wasn't for his advice, and some rigorous suggestions by my Reserve unit, this story would be very, very different.

So off I went to New York and the fun that is known as seasonal allergies. Here are the high points for my USMA experience: met great people, played baseball, was forcibly retired from baseball (i.e., cut from the team after a year), learned a ton, got aggressively mediocre grades, met my future wife, and commissioned as an officer in May of 2009. Again, leaving the West Point details for my future (non-existent) biographer.

I left West Point, got trained up on my military job as an armor officer, then to Fort Riley, Kansas. Three weeks after I got to Riley, I was in Iraq. I served in a staff role and got some incredible experience and did some great work bringing the unit's equipment home. I got home with a combat patch and prepared to take my next career steps. I also wanted to propose to my then-girlfriend, Drew, and so I did.

That very same night, on one of the most memorable evenings of our relationship, I made the dumbest mistake of my life. I drank too much and blacked out. I woke up in jail, arrested for being drunk and disorderly and resisting arrest. Instead of celebrating our engagement together, Drew was bailing me out of jail. Aside from putting her through this horrific event, I stared the end of my career in the face.

I earned every bit of anguish and suffering from that event, and for reasons unknown to me to this day, someone stepped in and said they'd be willing to let me stay. I was given a second life after several months of waiting with my future in the balance. I lived in shame for my actions that day for years, and it wasn't until much later did I close that chapter in my life. More on that in a bit.

Given that second chance was the greatest professional gift I have ever received. Without it, nothing that follows in this book would have happened. I wouldn't have gone to Afghanistan as a platoon leader, commanded a tank company in Korea, or met the incredible people at those jobs. I also wouldn't have been selected to return to West Point on the staff and faculty.

Shortly before returning to West Point, Drew and I had our first daughter, McKinley, and my world started to change drastically. I never understood the struggle or joy of having a child. I took for granted the pressure on a family. I also, really, REALLY missed sleeping in. (God bless parents—seriously.)

So many amazing people helped me get to West Point and returning there to earn my master's degree from Columbia was one of the proudest accomplishments of my life. While the material was incredible and I connected with it (and ultimately ended up working in the field), it was one class in particular that sticks with me to this day: LD740: Leader Development.

Aside from being a synthesis opportunity for the entirety of my grad school program, it was led by COL Everett Spain. To say that he had an incalculable impact on me is an understatement. One of the papers that we wrote was our "leadership journey," where we unpacked who we are as leaders. While I appreciated the reflective opportunity and chance to look at some of the more impactful, and even crucible-level, experiences in my life, it was the grade and feedback I received on that paper that struck me to my core.

"A-. You could have gone deeper."

I bore my soul in that paper, sharing my failures as a leader, and most importantly my arrest. The number of people who knew of that incident outside of my wife and the first unit I could count on one hand. I shared it in this paper, and in class. Who the hell was he to say I hadn't gone deep enough?

My reaction was, predictably, immature. Man-child, remember? But it ate at me.

After the arrest, I committed myself to becoming better as a person and a leader and focused on giving others second chances. I looked at my leadership through that lens and saw past initial mistakes to see potential in others.

Who was he to say I didn't go deeper?

Damn it, he was right.

That was a turning point for me. Well, a slow turning point, because it took another three years of COL Spain inviting me back to facilitate the crucible leadership lesson and allowing me to share my story. And being picked apart by the students, over and over again. Each time I shared that story and felt the shame all over again, he found another thread to pull.

"Have you spoken to the arresting officer since then?" Damn it, he was right.

See, after the initial arrest I searched for quite some time to find the name of the officer who arrested me to apologize. After quite some time he took my call, my apology, and later helped to make sure I wasn't prosecuted. He gave me a hug on that day in court and told me to pay it forward.

I thought that was it.

COL Spain's words ate at me. So, I found the officer again, and through our correspondence closed a gap in both of our hearts and stories. He had retired by that point; we emailed back and forth, but his words stuck with me. He told me he spent decades as a police officer, never really knowing if he made an impact. He said he cried when he read my letter, as it made him feel that he had indeed made an impact, even on one person.

The following year when I was invited back, I shared the story that the Kansas City Police Department wrote about the officer and my interaction. I felt like I was done, the chapter was finished.

"Have you ever talked with your family about the arrest?" Damn it!

I had always assumed my family knew or suspected. But I never talked about it with them. I was too ashamed. My mom was a police dispatcher for decades. My stepdad was a retired police chief and US Marshal. And I had been arrested, for an altercation with a cop.

So, I did. I talked with them about it. And wouldn't you know, they had no clue. That was a tough conversation, but more than ten years after the initial arrest, I felt like I could move past the incident. I learned that I can't hold on to those things. While I had outwardly used it for others to grow from through my poor example of character, I never actually allowed myself to forgive…myself.

The best way that I leverage that conversation now is that it is an incident that *informs* my leadership to this day, but it does not *define* me. Too often I find people who dwell on traumatic incidents and allow them to dictate their entire being. I won't ever forget that incident, but I have moved past it to become a better person. I think. I hope.

Let's get back on track so we can get into the transition. I moved into my role as a Company Tactical Officer (TAC) overseeing a cadet company at West Point. As a TAC, I was responsible for the leadership development of approximately 120 cadets. One day

I'd be inspecting how well someone did, or did not, make their bed, then the next I'd be helping someone navigate the stresses of losing a family member. It was a difficult, but rewarding job, serving as a coach and mentor for the cadets.

Unfortunately, I had to leave after a year to take a higher position overseeing nine of the companies. Telling my company that I was leaving after just a year was heartbreaking, as I grew to love them and their incredible spirits.

This jump catapulted me into an incredibly challenging position, and while I was hesitant to take it on. I had never intended to pursue one of the upper-tier leadership positions, I wanted to spend more focused time on a small group of future leaders. Even so, I enjoyed trying to help on a larger scale and being able to support more than 1,100 cadets.

It was at this point that I saw my wife and her professional challenges. She was a West Point graduate, earning her MBA at night, and working part-time. She was forgoing her professional aspirations to allow me to pursue mine.

That's when we decided to hang it up. Not because of ill will towards the Army, or that she wouldn't support me, but because I wanted to support her. I wanted our daughter (and later daughters) to see their mom succeed in her goals.

So, I told my bosses that I was leaving the army. They were supportive, if not a bit disappointed, but they understood my logic. I was lucky enough to find myself a full-time teaching position in the Department of Behavioral Sciences and Leadership at West Point teaching the Military Leadership course to the junior class. I spent my last year in the army teaching leadership at the most prestigious leadership development institution in the world. That's a hell of a résumé bullet if you ask me!

In December of my final year in the army, I did a full-court press in the transition. If I wasn't teaching, I was networking. If I wasn't doing something for the department, I was polishing my résumé. It was at this point I also started journaling on LinkedIn, in the hopes that I could help somebody else in their journey.

It also served as a method of public accountability. I am a chronic project starter, but I suffer from the inability to finish things. My logic was that if I put out my experience into the world, as well as my goals, the sheer embarrassment of failing to meet my metrics would keep me moving.

And, candidly, I was terrified about failing to find something meaningful after the army. Coincidentally, I learned that I was not alone in my feelings of fear and worry, something I would share with fellow transitioning service members after I made the jump.

Wouldn't you know, it worked. And as a happy little accident, it became my "brand." My network ballooned and people began following me for resources. I was able to share my findings in order to help others navigate the chaos. This process not only helped me leave the military in an intelligent way, but it also directly helped me find my first job. And not just a job to pay the bills, but something that excited me. Meaningful work that aligned with my purpose in life

So, let's see how I went about it.

The Journey:
A TWENTY-EIGHT-WEEK REFLECTIVE ADVENTURE

Post 1:
THE BEGINNING, BUT NOT THE START

Date: December 29, 2020

WHAT I DID THIS WEEK:
Created goal setting worksheet (Goal: Healthy Zach) using my own course material and a custom-designed worksheet I built last semester for my students and finished *Designing Your Life* and *Atomic Habits*. Cold-contacted HR reps in major Dallas companies (no return contacts yet). LinkedIn job research helped me narrow my focus to org dev (thanks "succession planning" search term!). Finished Hiring Our Heroes (HoH) application Phase 2. Thanks to my wife for proofreading!

WHAT I'M READING AND LEARNING:
Atomic Habits (complete). The concept of one percent better and small changes with a long-range view. Great book, highly recommend it. Started *At Ease* and *Grit*.

SELF-REFLECTION(S) OF THE WEEK:
Atomic Habits helped me realize a fatal flaw I have with my goals: when I fall off the horse, I fall hard. James brought up a great point: you will fail, but don't miss twice in a row. I fall into the trap constantly of saying, "Well, I failed this one time, guess I'm going to just give up." If I stumble, I'm going to pick myself up a lot quicker and get back on the horse.

DID I SUCCEED IN MY PREVIOUS GOAL(S):
I had created an amorphous goal of having one discussion per week with someone about transition, and I need to rework this leveraging my goal worksheet. I've succeeded overall, but I need to leverage some more effective goal-setting techniques to make things more tangible.

GOALS FOR NEXT WEEK:
Transition goal worksheet, have one discussion with a company HR representative, and begin Unqualified Resignation (UQR) paperwork.

GRATITUDE:

Thanks to Matt Rosebaugh for talking with me about life after transition and a position I was curious about. Thank you to Gina Buontempo for an awesome talk we had a couple of weeks ago about where Org Psych fits into the professional world.

IMPOSTER SYNDROME FIGHT: Other people already have jobs lined up, so why don't you?

REFLECTION QUESTION

In an ideal situation (not perfect), what does success look like for you at the end of your journey?

REFLECTION EXERCISE: WHO ARE YOU?

From my perspective, defining my purpose in life was the single most important part of my journey to learn who I am and what I want. There are many ways to go about this, but you should start by reading Nick Craig's book *Leading from Purpose* as a primer. Using his methods are incredibly helpful to flesh out your core purpose and define who you are.

To serve as a first exercise in this book, I want you to start by defining who you believe you are, right now. This is no small feat, to be fair. Let's scope it in quite a bit to help us set our footing, using the next page as a place to capture your thoughts.

When you think about your professional career accomplishments, what are you most proud of? This can be a single accomplishment, your body of work, whatever.

When you think about your personal life, what brings you the most joy? Is it your spouse, children, or other family members? Is it your activities? Where are your passions outside of the workplace?

If you had to capture a metaphor that speaks to your leadership style, what would it be? This can be very difficult for some people or incredibly easy for others. My friend Dr. Julia Sloan shared with me that this helps engage a different aspect of your thinking and can often serve as a rapid connection with others. For context, this is one of my favorite metaphors: I lead like I'm training a home cook to become a chef—different ingredients and techniques can come together and create something unique and delicious.

Now, let's make this difficult. In three sentences or less, who are you?

Not daunting at all, right? Nah, you'll be fine.

REFLECTION EXERCISE:
WHO ARE YOU?

What are you most proud of?

What brings you the most joy?

What is your leadership style metaphor?

Who are you?

Post 2:
NEW YEAR, BETTER ME

Date: January 8, 2021

WHAT I DID THIS WEEK:
Had a lot of work to get ahead on to prepare for my upcoming semester of teaching. Still had an awesome opportunity to learn about some "nudge technology" from one of the professors in my department, which I plan to implement in my classroom this semester to increase retention of subject matter. I also was fortunate enough to have a friend link me up with someone who works within a medium-sized consulting firm, and I had an awesome conversation with a veteran hiring manager within a large corporation. I finished the majority of my resignation paperwork and got some questions answered about how to set up my transition leave form. For my fellow vets who are thinking about the Career Skills Program (CSP), here are my general thoughts: it is extremely beneficial if you're looking to "intern" with a small company. However, in the multiple discussions I've had with large firms, they often do not take in unpaid interns, which is fundamentally

what the CSP role allows for. In all honesty, it ended up confusing most people I've talked to, but again if you're looking at a smaller organization or Hiring our Heroes, it's an awesome program. With that said, my wife and I have decided that I will forgo the CSP and jump straight into the market. I'll have ~120 days of terminal leave banked due to the pandemic, so I'm comfortable I'll find a great job with that much buffer.

WHAT I'M READING AND LEARNING:

Finished *Grit*. Dr. Duckworth works with my program, and I've always been fascinated with her work. There are so many powerful lessons to learn from her, but I loved the idea and story of job versus passion versus calling. Made me think more about what my true "calling" is and if I'm moving in the right direction. About halfway through *At Ease* and I really like this quote: "Don't look back. Don't run away from anything—run toward something."

SELF-REFLECTION(S) OF THE WEEK:

I need to answer the question of "Who am I?" in a concise manner (I'm thinking my personal elevator pitch). I've done this before, but I've grown so much since the last time I formalized and put into writing who I believe I am, so it feels relevant. Reading *At Ease* made me want to do a Bio Sketch that Rob outlines in the book, which I'll look to do in the coming weeks.

DID I SUCCEED IN MY PREVIOUS GOAL(S):

Yes and no. Successful in having at least one transition discussion, but I completely failed in doing my transition goal worksheet. I did maintain my "Healthy Zach" goal very well, so that's a plus. To be honest, I spent a lot of time watching the news this week with everything going on in the capitol, so I lost quite a few hours I planned on allocating to other endeavors.

GOALS FOR NEXT WEEK:

Transition goal worksheet, one discussion with a company HR representative, finish resignation paperwork, research Bio Sketch, and create a format.

GRATITUDE:

Thanks to Dr. Beth Wetzler for an awesome discussion about *Nudge* and Daniel Liss for thinking of me and getting me in touch with a friend of his to talk about opportunities in the private sector.

IMPOSTER SYNDROME FIGHT:

Elevator pitch? You can't put your experience into a 45-second speech; no one will understand it.

REFLECTION EXERCISE: ELEVATOR PITCH, VERSION 0.1

To this point, you've thought a bit about how you got to where you are, and ideally where you want to end up. Don't feel worried that you don't have this dialed in completely. When I went through the creation of my elevator pitch, it took me multiple iterations and practice sessions to feel comfortable pitching to people. But I'm perfectly fine making an ass of myself. It's a blessing and a curse. I need to swallow a bit of pride because I'm going to mess this up.

Reader, it's going to feel awkward practicing in front of a mirror. It's going to feel even more awkward when you share it with a prospective boss or a hiring manager. It's going to feel like a dagger in your chest when you screw it up. It's okay! We've all been there. They've all been there. Don't get dissuaded; keep at it.

I'm going to give you a very loose framework as a starting point and feel free to use the page at the end as a way to fill it in. Don't feel constrained by this, use it as a tool to adapt to your style. It needs to speak to you and feel authentic. From my standpoint, it should share with the person who you are in a succinct way that if they get it, they get you. If they don't, maybe it's not the right fit.

1. Positive opener and gratitude. Common sense but start off on the right foot and be thankful for the opportunity. Be excited but try not to come off as a crazy person.

2. Explain your relevant background and skills. Hit some key professional highlights. Bonus points if you've done your research ahead of time (you should), and tailor

some of your highlights to help address challenges at the organization you're talking with. Are they dealing with retention issues? Maybe talk about how you excelled at that and earned an award for doing so. If the company has specific education or training backgrounds, make sure to mention those. As an example, the company that ultimately hired me to serve as a leadership consultant appreciated my background in organizational psychology and my experience teaching leadership at West Point. Another suggestion is to create a list of these accomplishments, then boil them down into an easy-to-remember trigger for faster recall.

3. Make your story stick via a personal touch. Be authentic and truthful but share something that people will remember and lasts. Mine, for example, was that I was leaving the military to support my wife's career aspirations so my daughters could see their mom be successful in the workplace (which statistically speaking will make them more likely to succeed in the workplace as well). That's 100% true and I feel is memorable enough for someone to recall later.

4. Prepare your ask. I found this to be the most difficult part. Frankly, I still struggle with this in certain facets of my job, but I hate asking for help (it's a problem, I know!). But you need to think through what your "ask" is to this person. You've shared your story, so now what? So

what? Do you want to try and set up a time later to have coffee to learn more about their organization? Are you just looking for advice or mentorship? Do you want them to connect you with a hiring manager or someone who can discuss potential options? You need to think through your personal goal or outcome for the conversation.

5. Be gracious and thank them for their time. Be prepared, you might get shut down. The conversation might not go anywhere, they may not have anything available. They have still given you the gift of time and an opportunity to practice, so be thankful for that if nothing else.

Now you have a very loose framework that you can build using additional details and adapt based on the person you're talking with. If I was having a discussion over the phone or computer, I'd have my elevator pitch up to serve as a backup if I didn't remember it. I practiced with my wife and my coach. I rehearsed by myself. It felt *awkward*. You're boiling your life down into less than a minute to try and connect with someone and open a door to the next chapter of your life. It's a vulnerable thing, so do what you can to prepare yourself. You've got this! If I can do it, you definitely can, too.

And here's a little pro tip for you: write the person you talked to a thank-you note. Heck, do that for anyone you interview with. My friend Mark Raschke shared with me a story about his hiring process. He interviewed with a great organization and after he finished, he sat in their waiting room and wrote thank-you notes to everyone he talked with. Then, he gave them to the receptionist and asked that they be delivered. He was hired, and they specifically mentioned that the thank-you notes sealed the deal. At this point, Mark has been with that company for almost four years, and those people still have those notes. Don't discount the power of a handwritten thank-you note.

REFLECTION EXERCISE:
ELEVATOR PITCH V0.1

Positive opener and gratitude

Highlights
(use short reminder phrases)
1.
2.
3.
4.

Skills
1.
2.
3.
4.
5.
6.

Personal Story

The "Ask"

Gratitude!

Post 3:
PREP WORK

Date: January 15, 2021

WHAT I DID THIS WEEK:
I work on the Benavidez Leadership Development Program (BLDP), and the short version is that it's a three-week, graduate-level educational initiative for non-commissioned officers (NCOs). Because of the pandemic, we cannot work with our partners from Teachers College at Columbia University, so I've been working to put together an internally resourced program that matches the educational rigor that TC delivers. This week the pieces came together with funding approved (the last big hurdle), so now I just need to finalize some minor details before the 01FEB kickoff. I cannot wait to see what these NCOs do this year, because we're giving them some truly challenging change projects (their deliverables) to tackle. The work on BLDP, coupled with prep work for starting next semester, took up the bulk of the week.

In between, however, I was able to reconnect with old friends and acquaintances and finalize my Unqualified Resignation (UQR) paperwork! I'm just missing one memo, then I'll be complete. (Note: UQR is the formal term the military uses for an officer who decides to leave the service of their own volition, prior to retirement. By comparison, Qualified Resignations are those officers who resign in lieu of misconduct.)

I also spent a lot of time talking with peers about the attempted insurrection on January 6. I took the advice of one of my office mates and sent out a note to my former students and the rugby team that I mentor to let them know I'm here if they need to talk. I also built an MS Form to collect their feelings and how they would like staff and faculty to address the riots in the classroom. These are our future leaders who will shape the Army, and I want to have them talk through these problems in an open forum because I expect they'll be fixing them as officers.

WHAT I'M READING AND LEARNING:

Still working on *At Ease* and started *Invisible Women*. While I'm trying to focus my energy on transition-related books, I find so much value in reading things that challenge my worldview. So many valuable lessons from *Invisible Women*, many of which force me to think about how I can be a better, more inclusive leader. If you have an Audible subscription, the books are free as part of it, so please take the time to listen. It'll show you through data that the world isn't built with equality or equity in mind. I also learned about VA ratings, something I was completely ignorant about.

SELF-REFLECTION(S) OF THE WEEK:
Built a Bio Sketch and sent it to Rob, and he gave me some more feedback and homework. Expect a Human Needs evaluation of myself and more introspection in the future. In writing the Bio Sketch, I better realized that growth and learning are key parts of my life and I need to incorporate them into my job search.

DID I SUCCEED IN MY PREVIOUS GOAL(S):
Yes! Healthy Zach continues to rock (cut caloric intake from 1,800 down to 1,500-1,600 with an increased training regimen). Refined transition calendar, got in touch with multiple veteran assistance personnel, finished UQR (minus reserve memo), and created Bio Sketch.

GOALS FOR NEXT WEEK:
Consolidate info from cadet feedback about feelings and recommendations for addressing and share with key personnel to help improve dialogue in the classroom. Work on Human Needs evaluation. I already have multiple zoom calls scheduled throughout the week coupled with a return to teaching! I cannot wait to get back in the classroom. Most of my energy needs to focus on kicking off the semester strong for my students and finalizing details for BLDP, so a lot of my energy will shift away from transition until February. I've got a lot of evening calls set up, though!

GRATITUDE:

Thanks to Josh Kopsie for talking with me about his transition and getting me in touch with a VA rep and Rob Campbell for continuing to be an amazing mentor throughout this exciting period of my life. I also want to give a very special shout-out to Hamaria from Korn Ferry Advance. She is my educational and professional idol, and if I can achieve what she has in her life I'll be so fortunate. She is my KFA coach (we get three free sessions as part of the USMA AOG Career Services program), and recently she absolutely *shredded* my résumé in the absolute best way possible. She gave me some incredible feedback and resources to improve my résumé to put my best foot forward. She has been so incredibly helpful in my transition process, and I cannot thank her enough.

IMPOSTER SYNDROME FIGHT:

You don't have the skills necessary, and it's too late to get them.

REFLECTION EXERCISE: NEEDS SURVEY

This is a highly abbreviated version of Robert Kaufman's Needs Assessment. The overarching concept is that there is a difference between where you are and where you want to be. Doing a full Needs Assessment is intense but will give you some great information about your "gaps" to get to your next stage of life.

For our purposes, we're going to scope this in significantly with a Needs Survey focused on your professional career as you see it now and compare it to where you think you want to be. This can be a bit tricky and fuzzy because you might not have great clarity on your vision for your next life. That's okay because this will help you identify some important things. But critically, it will help you find some large gaps that you can start to fill.

For service members, there's an incredible resource available for you and your spouse: Syracuse University's Institute for Veterans & Military Families (https://ivmf.syracuse.edu/). Their Onward to Opportunity (O2O) program has some amazing offerings, but what sets them apart is their "Learning Pathways" program.

After applying, you can select one of a ton of courses, most of which after completion you earn an industry certification or credential. These range from IT-related training, Agile, PMP, and LSS. This is an insanely valuable benefit to your professional training, and something that can truly set you apart. As mentioned, however, the tricky part is finding out what to do.

Let me share a cautionary tale about why I'm an idiot. I wanted to set myself apart by becoming an Agile Certified Practitioner (PMI-ACP). I thought this would be a great way to add some additional depth to my résumé. How much research did I do as to what

Agile methodology was? Basically none. It wasn't PMP, so I was happy. This was a huge mistake. Not only was the program tailored for an industry I'll likely never work in, but I had little interest in the material. Worse, I waited too long in my transition process and was trying to do this course in the middle of trying to finish out teaching, packing, moving, and traveling cross country. Oh, and trying to find a job.

I was working hours a night to try to keep up. I was granted an extension (the O2O folks are super helpful and accommodating; they truly are amazing people), but then realized I was doing this for nothing. Even after I was hired by my current company, I kept working on this certification, purely out of pride.

Moral of the story: don't be like me. Put more thought into your selection and when you do this in your transition.

With that out of the way, let's get to work. I want you to take stock of the things tangible skills you have right now. Certifications, degrees, etc. Put those in the left-hand column. If you've started working on a résumé at this point, leverage this tool in two ways: to help you identify things to add to this, or potentially things to add to your résumé.

Now think through your experience. What tangible, measurable things can you *show*, with *specific examples* (numbers, dollar figures, etc.)? Do you have some volunteer info? Think deep. Add those into the left-hand column as well.

Let's get a bit more intangible. What types of soft skills do you have? These may not be as relevant to your résumé, but they might help you identify some things you enjoy. I'm a strong public speaker, for example, and it was important to me that I was able to leverage that in my next role. This can get a bit wishy-washy, but you're likely not sharing this with anyone who might hire you, so that's okay! Make sure to add these things to the left-hand column.

Get some feedback from a trusted advisor. What did you miss? More in this column is better, you can always cut it down later.

Now visualize your perfect future from a work standpoint. What is your job? What company are you working for? Can you research what it takes to be successful to help you identify what skills may be necessary for advancement? Try to give yourself a clearer picture of the jobs you might be a good candidate for. Put these visualizations into the right-hand column.

Now let's take the good to great.

Hop onto job boards or a big company's "Careers" page and find a role that you feel speaks to you, regardless of the company. (It could be a Human Resources Business Partner for JP Morgan Chase, for example.) Now look for similar jobs at other companies and start to take stock of the qualifications. Is there anything jumping to the forefront? Is there a credential that shows up frequently?

Now, search for people who fill those jobs on LinkedIn. Look at their certifications. Look at their training and job history. Identify as many themes as you can. It can be easy to get a bit frustrated here because they look so different to you. That's okay! They started from the bottom as well, you were just doing something else.

Start capturing the themes, certifications, or roles that you find. Put those in the middle column of your chart. Start to connect the dots between where you are to those things you found (your left column to your middle column). What reflections do you have? Do you have more connections than you realized? Less?

Take a look at your right column and connect those items to your middle column. Again, what reflections do you see? What's left over?

Analyze the info you have in front of you. When you look at the industry trends (middle column), what hasn't been connected at all? When you look at the left compared to the right column, what hasn't been connected through the middle column?

That's your gap as you see it now. The next question is tied to your specific journey: how do you fill that gap with something that makes you more marketable? Can you take a class or earn a certification that prepares you for your desired role, connecting more of your left and right columns together? Find the thing that is most impactful to set you apart.

Keep in mind, when you are hired, you will likely have ample opportunities for further training and development. If that's something important for you, make sure you ask questions about that during the hiring process. For example, I love to learn new things. I made sure to ask in interviews what opportunities for personal development were available. My company allows me to pursue additional training and certifications to keep me current and more effective in my role, which helps them be successful. I continue to build out my skills in an organization that supports me in the process. There are many organizations that do the same, so don't be too worried if your middle column seems daunting—you'll get there!

Before we move on, here's a big "bonus" step. Those people you found on LinkedIn are people you should try and connect with and talk to. There are opportunities to network and learn. They can show you what their day-to-day is like and if it's what you want to do. They might even be able to help you connect your previous work experience in a way that speaks to your desired goals and improves your hiring potential. I really should not put quotations around "bonus," because this is the technique that will set you apart, and it will give you more benefits than you realize right now.

Do it!

REFLECTION EXERCISE:
NEEDS SURVEY

SKILLS (TANGIBLE AND SOFT)

1.
2.
3.
4.
5.
6.
7.
8.
9.
10.
11.
12.
13.
14.
15.
16.
17.
18.
19.
20.
21.
22.
23.

TRENDS AND OBSERVATIONS

VISUALAIZED FUTURE STATE

Post 4:
PILING ON

Date: January 22, 2021

WHAT I DID THIS WEEK:

This week was an absolute grind fest. For transition-related things, I was able to meet with another veteran hiring manager, attended my Soldier For Life Transition Assistance Program (SFL TAP) pre-separation counseling, meet all the counseling required for the Reserves (I will not be involved with the Reserves in any capacity), and had an awesome discussion with an old friend. In between those events, I finally got to kick off the semester with my students. While doing classes remotely is not my favorite way to teach, the group I've got has been extremely engaged and I'm excited to go on this journey with them. I was incredibly impressed with their willingness to share their feelings about the riot on January 6. I learned a lot about their perspective and where their heads were during that time.

WHAT I'M READING AND LEARNING:

Reading took a back seat this week, unfortunately. Kids haven't been sleeping well (and by proxy neither have Drew and I), but I was able to listen to some more of *Invisible Women*. That book is really opening me up to biases in our culture that I was completely ignorant about. What really got me thinking is the "unpaid work" that women (largely) do, and how having children negatively impacts career progression. I'd like to think that we're getting better at supporting families to empower people to be in the workforce, but I suspect that it's not great. There's a lot that I'd hope to fix if given the opportunity.

SELF-REFLECTION(S) OF THE WEEK:

This seems silly, but as Drew and I have looked at houses, she sent me a beautiful one on a golf course. It made me think back to how much I value the sport and I think we may try to live nearby a course so we can (hopefully) get the kids involved! My grandparents lived on a golf course, and so much of my youth involved playing the game that I'd like to continue to cultivate that passion.

DID I SUCCEED IN MY PREVIOUS GOAL(S):

Holistically, no, but I'm not disappointed in myself for it. I was able to get some great feedback from previous students, and I feel like I started the semester off strong with my classes, but BLDP overtook me, and I was never able to get to the Human Needs evaluation. I'm hoping things calm down over the next couple of weeks so I can apply more energy to other endeavors.

GOALS FOR NEXT WEEK:
Finalize BLDP and teach with vigor! One of my favorite lessons, "Character and Its Development," comes up next week. I love that class and am excited to teach it to my students.

GRATITUDE:
Thanks to Brooke Jones for talking with me in between her crazy busy schedule! She's helping me get connected with some great people and it was fun to catch up with an old friend and classmate. Also, thanks to Nick Loudon for chatting with me all the way from Brazil. I met Nick through a family friend, and he walked the path I currently am a few years ahead of me. He was great about sharing his experiences prior to me arriving at West Point four years ago, and he was so gracious to provide me some insight to the professional world.

IMPOSTER SYNDROME FIGHT:
What are you running from?

REFLECTION QUESTION:
Take a look around your work, what inspires you the most?

Post 5:
INSPIRATION AND MOTIVATION

Date: January 29, 2021

WHAT I DID THIS WEEK:

This was a big week for the Benavidez Leadership Development Program. The BLDP Team continues to prep for our start on Monday, which has been a unique endeavor. Some amazing people stepped up to help. Also was able to talk with some great people in the industry, do a couple of transition classes (looking at you, financial planning class...), and have some tough conversations about biases, diversity, and sexual assault/harassment in the military. One of the contacts I made introduced me to the COMMIT Foundation, which I applied to and will meet with on Monday. Super excited to learn about them, as I had never heard of them prior to this week. I also met up with a former lieutenant from the unit I commanded and was so happy to hear about his journey through Ranger Regiment, command in the 82nd, and now his graduate school experience as he gets ready to be a TAC at West Point. I'm so proud of him and where he's going.

WHAT I'M READING AND LEARNING:

Was able to put some more time into the books, with a huge lesson learned from *At Ease* about celebrating your spouse. One of my primary reasons for getting out of the Army is to support my wife and her career aspirations, and that chapter really resonated with me. I also felt a strong link with *Invisible Women*, specifically the concept of "unpaid labor" that women do. I hope that I'm doing my part to carry that burden with my wife, and even if I have to take a back seat to let her drive the career bus, I'm happy to do so.

SELF-REFLECTION(S) OF THE WEEK:

Am I doing enough? I ask myself that a lot, and as I taught a class about perceptions and biases and shared some of my shortcomings, I find myself wondering if I am doing enough to help change the culture for the better.

DID I SUCCEED IN MY PREVIOUS GOAL(S):

Yes! BLDP is as finalized as it can be, and I feel like I left it all on the field for my lessons. I was also able to push through some transition classes and meet some amazing leaders working in the industry.

GOALS FOR NEXT WEEK:

I want to kick off BLDP strong, finish my financial planning course, finish At Ease, and meet with my COMMIT Foundation mentor.

INSPIRATION, PASSION, OR EXCITEMENT OF THE WEEK:

This is a new addition, courtesy of a conversation with Freddie Kim. He gave me some great no BS advice, which I found really refreshing and truly helpful. We talked a lot about how we define or redefine, ourselves, and the desire to make a difference in the civilian world. I found myself excited to fill a role with transitioning officers, not unlike the role others have filled with me. I know that I will miss the people in the Army when I head out, so this may be a healthy way for me to stay connected and feel like I'm making a positive impact. This was reinforced later in the week by S&P Global, specifically Adam Dikker. In a meeting about BLDP, I reached out to him for advice as a veteran who is transitioning. Within four hours he had senior S&P members from the NYC and Dallas offices chatting with me. I was so inspired by people willing to drop everything and help out, it was so fun to talk with these great people and learn about their experiences within the company.

GRATITUDE:

Thanks to Freddie Kim for talking with me, speaking to him was such a great experience and he gave me some no-BS advice and really reinforced that I've got to put in the work and prove myself in industry. Also, thanks so much to Adam Dikker for his incredible help, along with the rest of the folks within the VALOR group at S&P for their work with BLDP and taking the time to talk.

IMPOSTER SYNDROME FIGHT:
How can you possibly finish all of the things you need to do?

REFLECTION QUESTION:

What gives you inspiration and energy outside of the workplace? Are you a member of a team or organization? A church? Are you highly involved with your kids' sports?

_____
_____
_____
_____
_____
_____
_____
_____
_____
_____
_____

Post 6:
PUT IN THE WORK

Date: February 5, 2021

WHAT I DID THIS WEEK:

This week started off with a massive snowstorm, throwing the kickoff event for BLDP online at the last moment. We had to quickly pivot to remote instruction for the first two days, and slap together an online ceremony in the final hours. While it took some last-second cobbling together, I feel like it was an appropriate beginning to the program. It was also an absolutely wild week where I was introduced to so many amazing people and organizations and was accepted into a couple of incredible programs that provide Veteran assistance. Here's a quick rundown of the great opportunities out there that were brought to my attention:

> **Onward to Opportunity** (https://ivmf.syracuse.edu/programs/career-training/). Lots of great stuff going on here, but a tremendous resource for free certifications such as PMP and LSS to name a couple.

Candorful (https://candorful.org/about-us/). Does a ton of great stuff, but I plan on requesting assistance with interview practice and coaching.

ACP (https://www.acp-usa.org/). Pairs you with a fellow veteran mentor who has already transitioned. Super excited to learn more from my assigned mentor and become someone's protégé. They also offer active-duty spouse mentoring.

McKinsey Industry Insights (app and email). A helpful resource to understand and learn about different industries out there. Often, I feel like I'm looking at hieroglyphics, which I can imagine is what people looking at Version 1.0 of my résumé were feeling.

One of the most exciting agencies I started working with is the COMMIT foundation. The initial meeting struck all the right chords with me, and they assigned me a coach to help me define who I am. I am absolutely pumped to do a deep dive into where I'm at right now as I fully believe this will give me an incredible foundation to where I want to go. I absolutely love serving as a coach and having so many opportunities to be on the receiving end is amazing. I look forward to taking this head-on.

Early in the week, I was able to do my annual discussion with the incoming Eisenhower Leadership Development Program team. I share a story of a personal failure and lapse in character that helps frame crucibles for their grad school lesson, and I'm able to share additional lessons learned from my experiences at West Point. I'm so thankful to work with them and will miss that when I'm gone! This week also kicked off my return to in-person instruction, which really made my week even better. There's nothing like talking leadership with eager young leaders in the room.

WHAT I'M READING AND LEARNING:

Taking a key from Joe Byerly, I have been reading early in the morning (my wife's alarm goes off at 5 a.m., and mine at 5:45, so I usually have 40 or so minutes to read unless the kids wake up). I finally finished *At Ease*, and I highly recommend the book to transitioning veterans. While there are times when the gap between Rob and me seems vast (such as the age difference between our kids), the emotions he experienced and shared have resonated with me deeply.

SELF-REFLECTION(S) OF THE WEEK:

Put in the work. To date, I have made 19 different note-taking documents with reflections from meetings/discussions I've had. I had to create a separate document for "Stuff to Research" which consists of industries, companies, and concepts to learn more about. Each conversation opens new doors and sends me down new and fun rabbit holes. I have a sneaking suspicion that what I'm doing is the "right answer," but I must caution anyone about making the leap: you must put in the work. I'll keep you all posted if it pays off, but I truly believe it will. After talking with Tim Dunn, he made a great link for me and I think it's meaningful to share: You must find the overlap between "What do I bring to the table, the demand in the market, and which industries interest me." I put this idea into a Venn Diagram as I now have a bullseye to shoot for.

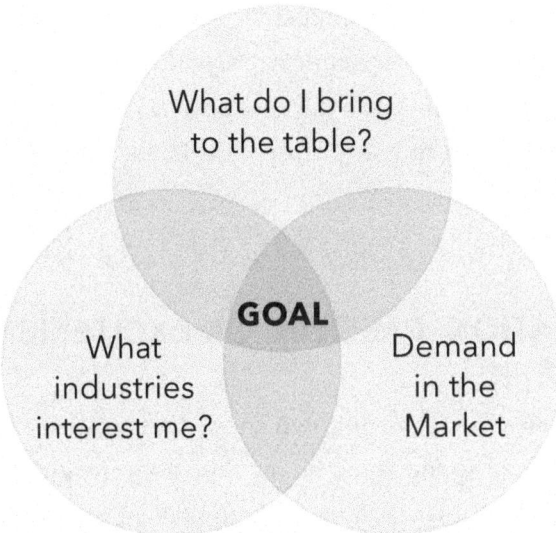

DID I SUCCEED IN MY PREVIOUS GOAL(S):
Almost. BLDP started off great and continues to drive forward, At Ease is done, and I met with COMMIT. I never got around to finishing the financial planning course. I might be able to sneak it in by this evening, but I'm not rushing to failure with that class.

GOALS FOR NEXT WEEK:

Huge week for teaching, need to put my energy there. Also need to finalize details for BLDP graduation to help the program finish strong, plus finish financial planning. I'll be meeting with my COMMIT Coach, a résumé coach, and will try and meet with at least one member from industry. Not sure how much time I'll have to dedicate to other endeavors, will likely be a light week for transition goals. I need to survive until 25 February when BLDP is complete then I'm going truly hard in the paint into transition tasks.

INSPIRATION, PASSION, OR EXCITEMENT OF THE WEEK:

Two big ones. First, having two snow days to start the week gave me a chance to spend some bonus time with my girls. While I was still doing a lot of work, being able to take a break and go sledding was very special. Second, the cadets I mentor continue to inspire me. I've been working very closely with quite a few cadets for various reasons, and I find myself so energized when I get to meet with them. They're like sponges, and I hope I'm giving them good advice.

GRATITUDE:

Thanks to Reggie Mills for getting me absolutely amped up for transition. He was so fun to talk to and learning about COMMIT was just so invigorating. Thanks to Bethany Biszko for talking to me about what it's like to work inside S&P and provide some amazing tips to set myself apart. Also huge thanks to Jason Wright for keeping an eye out for me and stepping up for a fellow vet. Tim Dunn was a blast to talk with and gave me some rock-solid advice to propel me into another level of learning about my path. Finally, biggest shout out to my wife, Drew. Her 35th birthday is coming up, and as we head towards our tenth anniversary, I find myself so lucky to have her in my life. She keeps me honest, challenges me to be a better person, and is an amazing mother to our children. I can't wait to take the next step in our journey together.

IMPOSTER SYNDROME FIGHT:
What if you can't make ends meet when you leave?

REFLECTION EXERCISE: WHAT ARE YOUR EMPLOYMENT REQUIREMENTS?

This is not an exhaustive list, but rather an opportunity to prime your brain into thinking through things that are important to you in your next role. If you identify other key aspects to your requirement, add them in. This is your journey, take the wheel and drive!

Pay: What's your range? Here's a starting point: what's your current compensation? Figure that out in depth and use it as a starting point. If it's your first time going to a new industry, shoot for at least the same quality of living.

Military folks, keep in mind VA benefits may help, but healthcare costs could be more than $1,000 a month for a family, and you'll have to pay out of pocket until you reach your deductible. It's a bigger monetary hit than I realized when I left. Also, the earliest you will get your VA rating is on your separation date, and for some it could take months before you're notified, and even longer to start payments. Plan for the worst-case scenario but hope for the best (just don't bank on it).

There are far more qualified people than me to talk through budgeting, but here's some things to keep in mind.

- Look at your household income now and what you're projected to make.

- Think through the potential costs, and research the new costs you might not be used to, such as a mortgage or medical/dental/vision.

- Build a comprehensive budget so you have a better understanding of your financial situation. It won't be perfect, but it can give you some understanding of what you need to make to live the life you want.

- Remember that there's the opportunity for advancement, bonuses, and other compensation that might cover potential pay cuts. During discussions with potential employers, make sure you ask questions around these if they're important to you. It can be daunting but ask the questions!

Flexibility: Remote? In-person? Hybrid? Travel? Or put another way: how much would you be willing to pay to get the flexibility you want? Some organizations treat remote or hybrid work as a "benefit." Keep that in mind.

Performance and Advancement: Are you comfortable with a slower advancement schedule? Or do you want to rapidly move if you put in the extra time? Make sure you think this through, there's costs and benefits to both. If you expect to be rewarded for going above and beyond but your organization is very time-based in their promotion structure, you might be a bit frustrated.

Role: Is there a specific thing you want to do? Are you an engineer who wants to work in a very specific field? Do you want to work for a company that does job rotation to allow you to test things out? There's a ton of options out there if you ask.

Experience: What are you trying to get out of the time in this job? Is it a steppingstone to get your feet into industry? Is it a very difficult role that will supercharge your growth in a short period of time? Do you just want stability and draw a paycheck to allow you to pursue other endeavors outside of the workplace?

Training and Development: Do you want the ability to pursue self-development? Do you want to get an advanced degree? Does your company support that with time and/or money?

Mentorship and Coaching: What systems do you want for an organizational mentorship plan? Does this even matter to you? Do they have an internal coaching program through their HR team that can help you improve? If this is important to you, make sure you poke around for what's available.

Culture: How important is the culture to you? This is one of the more difficult things to assess, because often you can't tell until you've been there for a while. If you get the opportunity to see the organization beforehand, compare what they say versus what you see. Strong organizational cultures will wear that on their sleeve, and you'll see it everywhere. It can feel almost cult-like at times. Don't be afraid to look at mission, vision, and principles pages on company websites to find something that resonates with you. If you see something important to you, don't be afraid to ask culture-related questions during the networking and/or interview process.

I won't dive too much deeper into the culture game because it's too vast to tackle in this context. I've spent years studying the concept and there's hundreds, if not thousands, of books written on the topic, and yet I still feel like an amateur in the field. Just keep in mind that if culture matters to you, do your homework, and make sure it's a good fit.

REFLECTION EXERCISE:
EMPLOYMENT REQUIREMENTS

Compensation Expectations	WHY	
Flexibility	WHY	
Performance → Advancement	WHY	
Role	WHY	
Experience	WHY	
Training and Development	WHY	
Mentorship and Coaching	WHY	
Culture	WHY	

Post 7:
STARTING TO FEEL REAL

Date: February 12, 2021

WHAT I DID THIS WEEK:

This was a busy week full of a lot of fun and exciting conversations, and everything is feeling more tangible. On top of teaching nine class periods and facilitating a character development session, I was able to meet with my new executive coach, Kyle. I am beyond excited to work with him and leverage the Pursuing Your Purpose material with the COMMIT foundation. I've got a lot of homework to keep on track but having an accountability partner is a very powerful motivator. I also had the privilege to work with Scott Vedder on my résumé, and he gave me so many amazing nuggets to help me improve my marketability that I cannot thank him enough (*love* the "Smarter than a 5th-Grader Test"). One of the chance encounters I had was courtesy of my wife meeting Donnie LaGrange. He invited us to a Joint Service Academy Networking event, and the amazing discussions, connections, and resources they helped us with are incredible. Having allies in the DFW area looking out for us is so comforting and we're very grateful. One of those connections is helping us with the VA Loan process, which is super helpful, and we're also working with a financial planner to help us understand a lot of the other unknowns out there. It was a big week for putting on adult pants.

Another really meaningful conversation came from Rob Stanton. He walked the path I'm on not too long ago, with the same reasoning for leaving the Army. He gave me so many great bits of advice and wisdom about where he ended up and how is military experience translated well (and not so well) to compensation. He helped validate many of the things that I'm actively doing and helped me "put teeth" into some other amorphous ideas I've kept in the ether (such as when I shift from my learning phase to my hunting phase). He helped me understand that at some point I need to have an "ask" for the conversations I'm having, and I plan on going into each discussion with that idea in mind. He also gave me a great way to think about the transition like a tricycle. The three wheels are: where I want to go (location), what I want to do (job), and how much money I want to make. Of those three wheels, one is the largest and drives the other two. My wife and I started briefly discussing which one is our biggest wheel, so more to follow on that...

It was also Drew's birthday this week, so we took some time to make a tasty dinner (homemade pot stickers and cheesy ramen) to celebrate!

WHAT I'M READING AND LEARNING:
Nearly complete with *Invisible Women* and started Adam Grant's *Think Again.* I use a lot of concepts from his podcast and writings in my class, so I'm excited to go through his newest book. I keep learning so much about how little data and information we have about women and seeing the jobs report from a couple of weeks ago where it was 100% women losing their job really made me want to be in the position to do more to fix that problem.

SELF-REFLECTION(S) OF THE WEEK:
I ran down to work with the rugby team that I help mentor, and at the start of practice one of the players started off the day talking about what gives him goosebumps. Then the coach asked me to share with the whole team. As I briefly thought about it, my only answer was them. They are a phenomenal group of young men who care deeply about developing their character. They make mistakes, but they own them, and I'm so fortunate to work with them. They use the sport as an avenue to become better people, and that's why I get goosebumps just being around them. As I ran back home, I reflected on how much I'll miss them and how important being around a high-performing and caring group of people means to me. I hope to find…or create…that wherever I end up next.

DID I SUCCEED IN MY PREVIOUS GOAL(S):
Details are nearly complete for the BLDP graduation, and we will have the Sergeant Major of the Army joining for a few hours to

hear project presentations (big win!). I'm super excited to see the hard work of these NCOs viewed at the highest levels of the Army. I did end up finishing the financial planning course in time, and that has helped me set the stage with my financial planning team. I met with so many great people, and absolutely crushed my goals. That tells me I need to step up my game...

GOALS FOR NEXT WEEK:

Enjoy the long weekend with the kids. Learn from the great meetings I have lined up. Complete COMMIT Modules 1-4 (and associated homework), refine my résumé using Scott's tips, and complete my financial planning worksheet. Need to start workshopping a handover plan for my responsibilities with the rugby team, may put a lot of energy to that in two weeks. I also have to put a few hours into my family's website, I'm tasked with updating it and really want to get it back online.

INSPIRATION, PASSION, OR EXCITEMENT OF THE WEEK:

I had two of the rugby players approach me before practice about some great news and I was thankful to have been a part of their development. Also talking with the coaching staff was so invigorating, they always bring the energy and make me want to go run into people!

GRATITUDE:

So thankful for Kyle Moses and Scott Vedder, two amazing people that the COMMIT foundation is enabling me to work with. Huge thank you to Donnie LaGrange and the JSAN team who spent so much time talking with me and Drew and opening their arms wide to bring us in. Rick Garcia put together an amazing assessment for us in record time so we can understand the costs associated with purchasing a new home. Thanks to Rob Campbell for getting me in touch with Rob Stanton, and Rob Stanton for his incredible words of wisdom. Our career paths were nearly identical (except he made it through BN command and to retirement) and it was so great to hear from someone who tread that ground and has been very successful.

IMPOSTER SYNDROME FIGHT:

How can you possibly find happiness after you leave?

REFLECTION QUESTION:

To paraphrase the quote from *At Ease* by my friend COL(R) Rob Campbell: What are you running toward?

Post 8:
CAREER HIGHLIGHTS

Date: February 19, 2021

WHAT I DID THIS WEEK:

This was a busy week. Between the weather forcing BLDP online for the majority of the week, coupled with a busy teaching schedule, I felt like I had little time to put energy to the transition. I was able to complete the first four modules for the COMMIT foundation in preparation for my next coaching session, which caused me to reflect quite a bit on my values. One of the big lessons I've taken away from the training and talking with multiple people is that if my values aren't aligned with the organization I'm working with, then I'll be unhappy and drained. The challenge for most of us, in my opinion, is that we don't actually know what our values are. As I refine my values further, I keep coming back to Justice, Teamwork, and Growth. Those have popped up multiple times throughout various assessments I've done in the past four years, and I look forward to dialing them in to align with a future organization I will work for.

I was able to have some unique engagements this week, engagements that were very meaningful. I was fortunate enough to have an assistant teacher join me as I covered for another professor for our humility lesson. Leveraging Brennan's experience and viewpoint was so awesome, and it was a blast to have him. Additionally, one of my grad-school buddies and current TAC Ross joined in to help me teach Transformational Leadership. He just defended his dissertation on TFL, so it was amazing to have someone with that level of experience in the classroom.

I was also able to meet with Brandon, the CEO of Beanie and Blazer. Learning more about his story, his company, and what they're doing was not only super intriguing, but also motivating. I feel like I bring a lot of energy and optimism to my life, but Brandon took it a step further and got me all amped up. I look forward to nurturing our friendship and I hope to provide some value to his goals in the future!

Carrying the heavy workload this week was my wife. Despite the struggles I felt, she was at home dealing with two kids while I was at work teaching. This continues to reinforce the importance to me that I need to put her career choices ahead of mine for our next step, as she continues to support me in ways for which I can't begin to thank her enough.

WHAT I'M READING AND LEARNING:

I have been crushed with BLDP and other late-night events, so I have failed to keep up on the reading side of things. I also got another book from my coach, Kyle, that I need to add into the fray as well! BLDP graduates next week, so I need to stop being lazy and get my nose back in the books.

SELF-REFLECTION(S) OF THE WEEK:
As I was teaching humility this week to my students, I realized how much tension exists with my desire to stay humble by the necessity to "sell myself" via a résumé or interview. I'm going to have to come to terms with talking more openly about my accomplishments, as I'm so used to downplaying my role in things.

DID I SUCCEED IN MY PREVIOUS GOAL(S):
I have not refined my résumé to the depth that I wanted to, nor did I have a chance to work on the website. Losing multiple days due to weather meant being present for my kids as much as possible. Hoping to carve out that time next week! Otherwise, I was able to complete everything else that I needed to ensure I stay on track with my Pursue Your Purpose Modules with COMMIT.

GOALS FOR NEXT WEEK:
Graduate BLDP, finalize rugby plan, work on the website, grow from coaching, and attend our department "Back Porch" event on Friday. I did my evaluation counseling with my senior rater last week, and I identified my lack of involvement with department activities as a failure, so he challenged me to stretch my legs more.

INSPIRATION, PASSION, OR THE EXCITEMENT OF THE WEEK:

So many things this week, but I'll speak to the power of just one. In partnership with S&P Global, which has a habitual relationship with BLDP, I was able to participate in an event with Yvette Benavidez Garcia, the daughter of MSG Roy Benavidez, Medal of Honor Recipient. I came into the Army as a PV2 in 2005, and in the back of my "smart book" was MSG Benavidez's story. I became enamored with it. When I was asked to be a part of the Benavidez Leader Development Program, named in his honor, I jumped at the chance. As I've learned more about his life and his dedication to this country and education (he was unable to attend school but was still a brilliant linguist, among many things), I've also learned about his long-lasting connection with West Point. Being on a zoom call with the BLDP NCOs, S&P, and Mrs. Benavidez was a high point of my career. I feel like we try to honor his legacy with the program, and I believe he would've been proud to see what came together last night.

GRATITUDE:

Thank you to Brennan and Ross for helping me teach this week, it was a blast to learn from your styles and perspective. Thank you to Brandon for firing me up about team building and personal development. Thank you to S&P VALOR, specifically Adam, for his care for our program and for bringing us together for the event last night. And last, and most importantly to me this week, thank you to Yvette. It was so wonderful to hear about her experience not only with her father but about her journey to live a life in line with his vision for this country. He embodied the American Dream, and despite a legendary career filled with unrivaled successes, I'd argue that his greatest accomplishment lives on through her and the values she exemplifies.

IMPOSTER SYNDROME FIGHT:

There's no way you can find satisfaction after you leave. It's impossible because you aren't talented enough.

REFLECTION QUESTION:

What was the most rewarding experience in your professional career to this point?

Post 9:
CULMINATING EVENT

Date: February 26, 2021

WHAT I DID THIS WEEK:

BLDP is finished. After a crushing few months, we graduated twenty-four non-commissioned officers from the program. At times it felt like it would never end, but I'm so proud of how it finished. The change projects that the NCO groups presented were outstanding, and the graduation ceremony was next level. My team and I were able to orchestrate what I believe was a top-notch and meaningful ceremony. The header photo was the night before when we had the venue set up, and the photo below is from my seat in the back where I was working the AV and with the broadcast team during the event. It felt so amazing to see the work go into an event that went so smoothly and had many meaningful portions. It's hard to put into words how amazing the event was, if you'd like to see it for yourself, as of the time of this writing, the link is here: https://youtu.be/KYEjdgEXDkw

Early in the week, I had an awesome conversation with Kate, and she was so helpful in wanting to lend a hand to a fellow veteran. I look forward to learning more from her and staying in touch in the future. She also got me in touch with some other people, from whom I am so excited to learn as well.

I also had my second coaching session where Kyle and I discussed my states of flow, and I'm learning more that I excel at balancing multiple things. However, I need to improve my ability to focus on tasks, as I often feel like the prototypical "jack of all trades, master of none." I believe my professional experience has led me to learn fast and move on, because the longest position I have held is seventeen months, and that was split between two countries.

Finally, I met John, who opened his heart and Texas network to me and Drew. Hearing his story was truly inspiring, and I look forward to learning more from him.

WHAT I'M READING AND LEARNING:

I've learned a ton, but unfortunately not from reading this week. I was re-introduced (embarrassingly!) to Dr. Brené Brown's work with vulnerability through the *WorkLife with Adam Grant* podcast. I was familiar with it but never dove into her work, which I plan to do. Learning more about the concept of vulnerability through her example is something I want to explore, as I've been testing it myself in the last few years. I've learned that vulnerability is often misconstrued as weakness, but that's extremely wrong. There is no courage without vulnerability, and I love helping people understand that concept. I was able to start BG(R) Seidule's book *Robert E. Lee and Me*. I had the good fortune to have him as a professor during grad school and hearing the fruits of his labor has been a lot of fun.

SELF-REFLECTION(S) OF THE WEEK:

I find more and more that I cope with stress and celebrate through eating. While my health has ebbed and flowed, yet largely remained in decent "Army Shape," the stress of the last two weeks derailed my Healthy Zach goal. I need to decouple food (and beer!) from those facets of my life and establish a better connection to reduce the chance that I'll fall off the wagon with my health goals.

DID I SUCCEED IN MY PREVIOUS GOAL(S):

All but working on the website! I may be able to sneak an hour into it after I publish this article, but no guarantees. There were some really meaningful events that hopped on my Friday calendar that I wanted to participate in.

GOALS FOR NEXT WEEK:

Take a brief pause to reset and refocus. I have a heavy teaching load next week, coupled with grading papers, so I'm putting my energy there. The only other goal I have is to complete the lodge website so that we can bring it back online. Otherwise, I'm keeping my schedule mostly open so I can grade papers and take care of some personal/family things.

INSPIRATION, PASSION, OR EXCITEMENT OF THE WEEK:

One of my students approached me after class and mentioned that they shared some deeply personal facets of their life in the paper they just submitted. They also mentioned that they had never spoken of the events before. I was so thankful to them for their willingness to be courageous and vulnerable, and I was very happy that they felt comfortable opening up to me and sharing. Those little connections are so inspiring, and I truly hope that I'm able to help them process those events and grow into better leaders.

GRATITUDE:

Thank you to the BLDP support team, Donnie Seidle and Shawn Robertson, for doing some serious heavy lifting to help the program across the finish line. Thank you and congrats to my good friend Josh Bowen for earning the best professor award for BLDP, and for his tremendous help with the program over the last three years. Thanks to Kate Migliaro for taking the time to chat with me, and for her desire to help other veterans. Thank you to John Roper for his inspirational story and for opening his heart up to us. Last, thanks to COL Everett Spain for getting me in touch with John, and his continued role modeling of the power of vulnerability. He pushes me and himself on this at every opportunity to continue to grow into a better person and leader.

IMPOSTER SYNDROME FIGHT:

You won't find the same level of happiness in your new life because it doesn't exist for you.

REFLECTION EXERCISE: BACKWARDS PLANNING 101

It's tough to capture over a decade's worth of military training and experience in how to backward plan in a short, but meaningful exercise. But you know what they say about excuses, right?

Let's start with some terms to make sure we're on the same page. Some of these may not be applicable outside of the military, but I'm hopeful they'll be useful in some capacity for you.

- **Transition date:** The day you want to start your new life/career.

- **Separation date:** The day you no longer have the pay/benefits from your previous job.

- **Relocation date:** The day you pick up and drive away from your previous location (if applicable).

Unless you're retiring and/or planning on taking some extra time off (which is great!), for most the goal is to have employment before your separation date. When I built the first version of my calendar, I had the mark on the wall of starting a new job by July 5, 2021, with basically no time off. I realized throughout my journey that I needed some time to myself, so I took an extra month to figure things out. This still gave me plenty of time prior to my separation date, and I had about six weeks of "double-dipping" paychecks, which was a nice little boost to the saving prior to leaving the army.

For everyone, don't forget to think through:

- Kids' school finishing (and registering for the next school)
- Childcare
- Utilities off/on
- Scheduling movers
- Renting or purchasing a home

For the service members, here are some other critical things to think about:

- VA appointments (you can do these during terminal leave, which is what I did)
- HHG movement
- College applications & GI Bill stuff (if applicable)
- Clearing post activities
- PTDY days (only if retiring)

Okay, so I've now thrown a bunch of stuff at you. We'll call those your key tasks. Let's start to lay it all out on a calendar.

Start with the furthest date in the future with the Transition, Separation, and Relocation dates. For most, that will be your separation date. For transitioning service members, this is a big deal. This will be your last paycheck from the government. And, even more importantly, your last day of healthcare coverage for you and your family. I could go on a rant about this for days, but it boils down to this: paying for healthcare sucks.

I'm an Excel junkie, so I built a calendar that counted down the days for me. It also allowed me to put in the key events, by day, for my job and other responsibilities to show me the free time I had to focus on transition tasks:

Date	DOW	Days Til Start	Task	Date	DOW	Days Til Start	Task
1-Feb-21	MON	154	BLDP	1-Mar-21	MON	126	Teach/ Grade
2-Feb-21	TUE	153	ELDP	2-Mar-21	TUE	125	Grade
3-Feb-21	WED	152	BLDP	3-Mar-21	WED	124	Teach/ Grade
4-Feb-21	THU	151	Teach	4-Mar-21	THU	123	Grade
5-Feb-21	FRI	150	On Call Funeral	5-Mar-21	FRI	122	Teach/ Grade
6-Feb-21	SAT	149		6-Mar-21	SAT	121	
7-Feb-21	SUN	148		7-Mar-21	SUN	120	
8-Feb-21	MON	147	Teach	8-Mar-21	MON	119	Notify BBC
9-Feb-21	TUE	146	BLDP	9-Mar-21	TUE	118	
10-Feb-21	WED	145	Teach + LC TTT	10-Mar-21	WED	117	
11-Feb-21	THU	144	BLDP	11-Mar-21	THU	116	Teach + On Call Funeral
12-Feb-21	FRI	143	Teach + LC	12-Mar-21	FRI	115	
13-Feb-21	SAT	142		13-Mar-21	SAT	114	
14-Feb-21	SUN	141		14-Mar-21	SUN	113	
15-Feb-21	MON	140	BLDP	15-Mar-21	MON	112	Teach + LC2 RxL
16-Feb-21	TUE	139	BLDP	16-Mar-21	TUE	111	
17-Feb-21	WED	138	Teach	17-Mar-21	WED	110	Teach + LC2
18-Feb-21	THU	137	BLDP	18-Mar-21	THU	109	
19-Feb-21	FRI	136	Teach	19-Mar-21	FRI	108	Teach
20-Feb-21	SAT	135		20-Mar-21	SAT	107	
21-Feb-21	SUN	134		21-Mar-21	SUN	106	
22-Feb-21	MON	133	JL Due	22-Mar-21	MON	105	Contact William
23-Feb-21	TUE	132	BLDP Projects / Grade	23-Mar-21	TUE	104	
24-Feb-21	WED	131	BLDP Grad / Grade	24-Mar-21	WED	103	WPR
25-Feb-21	THU	130	Teach / Grade	25-Mar-21	THU	102	Teach / Grade
26-Feb-21	FRI	129	Schedule HHG / Grade	26-Mar-21	FRI	101	Grade
27-Feb-21	SAT	128	Grade	27-Mar-21	SAT	100	Grade

Use the method that best works for you. A hand-held planner, desk calendar, whatever. Make it easy for you to access, update, and actually use. Block off the weekends, unless it's something you absolutely know you'll be doing on a Saturday or Sunday. Add in all your key tasks, and if necessary, think through how long you think they will take. For example, how long will it take to pack up? On that note, when are you calling the moving company to schedule that? Or are you moving by yourself? Do you need to get a truck?

You can start to see the value of backward planning. But this is a good time to bring up two fundamental truths of planning: 1) you can't forecast everything, and 2) don't fill up the entire calendar. Those are closely connected, because if you try to jam every minute of your calendar with tasks to accomplish, something is going to go awry, and your plan starts to derail. Build some space into your calendar to allow for mistakes and breathing room.

Add as much detail as you can, but don't feel like it has to be perfect. Again, things are going to pop up unexpectedly, but that's okay! You've planned for this and thought that through. You'll start to see how much, or little, free space you have available. For me, that was my networking time. Seeing how much time I had motivated me to create networking goals. Depending on how far out you are, this might give you anxiety. You've got this!

REFLECTION EXERCISE:
BACKWARDS PLANNING 101

Transition Date	Separation Date	Relocation Date

List of Key Tasks

Method I will use to build my calendar

Post 10:
RECHARGE THE BATTERIES

Date: March 5, 2021

WHAT I DID THIS WEEK:

Slow week this week from a transition standpoint. Needed to catch up on grading papers and put my energy into the classroom. I was, however, able to make some awesome connections. I had an amazing talk with Carrie, who shed some light on working inside a boutique consulting firm. It was really enjoyable talking with her and learning more about some of the specifics of her organization. I also got to meet my ACP mentor, Neil. It was a lot of fun getting to talk with him and establish a long-term relationship as I go through, and beyond, my transition. I also made an executive decision to get some new suits; hopefully, they end up fitting well and looking professional! I also had a chance to reconnect with Brandon and talk with him some more, and hopefully, he'll be joining me as a guest lecturer in my classroom!

WHAT I'M READING AND LEARNING:

I was able to pick back up with *Think Again* by Adam Grant and listen to *Robert E. Lee and Me*. Between the youngest kiddo deciding to wake up at 5 a.m. (my normal reading time) this week and working in the evening grading, I haven't spent a lot of time in the books.

SELF-REFLECTION(S) OF THE WEEK:

I find myself feeling less anxious than I expected I would at this stage in the transition. Maybe that will change, but I'm starting to feel prepared to make the jump. I still have so much work to do, and it does feel overwhelming at times, but I am confident in the path I'm taking and that it will pay off in the long run.

DID I SUCCEED IN MY PREVIOUS GOAL(S):

Yes, and I got the website back online as well! Feel free to check it out at highlakelodge.com. I still have a lot of work to do, but I wanted to have it back up for potential clients to access.

GOALS FOR NEXT WEEK:

Enjoy the weekend with the family. The weather looks cold but sunny, so hopefully, it'll be some quality outside time! I also want to complete grading by Wednesday evening, finish my taxes, and finish up COMMIT Modules 5-8. I've got to keep grinding away at a lot of different competing priorities to stay ahead of the game.

INSPIRATION, PASSION, OR EXCITEMENT OF THE WEEK:

The paper I'm grading is called *The Journey Line*. We use this as a tool to get cadets to reflect on developmental experiences in their lives that helped shape core values, ultimately to answer the question "What is my purpose in life?" So many of the stories they share are incredible, inspiring, and heartbreaking. This semester my students put their soul into this assignment, and while it has been difficult to read them at times, it has been an honor to do so.

GRATITUDE:

Thank you to ACP and my new mentor, Neil. Thank you to Carrie for taking the time to chat with me so I could learn from her incredible experiences. Thanks to Brandon for the follow-up chat. Thank you to Seidule for his incredible book. To be fair, though, I did get some early "free chicken" to some of the subject matter. But it is awesome to hear his voice again!

IMPOSTER SYNDROME FIGHT:

How can you possibly find new friendships? You're too different from anyone else in your next career.

REFLECTION QUESTION:

What worries you the most about the next steps?

Post 11
ASKING FOR HELP

Date: March 12, 2021

WHAT I DID THIS WEEK:

This was a busy one, despite only teaching one day this week. I was able to grade and provide ample feedback for my students, mentor a few cadets, and had the honor to support the funeral of a 90-year-old Korean War Veteran. I also hopped into the monthly service academy networking event for the Dallas area and was greeted again with open arms. A couple of the members provided me with some help after the meeting on my résumé and some other advice about the local area. It is always so wonderful to have a support network and I'm very thankful for these great people.

I also had the opportunity to learn more about Sales Platoon, who brought me in to listen to Rod Hairston (CEO of Growth-U) which was very inspiring. While I'm not interested in pursuing sales as a job after I leave the military, it is a great avenue for transitioning military to jump into. If you have some serious hustle, please take a look at https://www.salesplatoon.org/. There's so much great experience, not necessarily sales-specific, that you can gain from working with Sale Platoon. As a huge bonus, they work in tandem with the "Hiring Our Heroes" corporate fellowship program, so it's an easy fit with a transitioning service member. You can also stick with Sales Platoon or get hired as an account executive elsewhere.

Some of the key lessons I got from the lunch meeting with Rod and the discussion with Chris afterward were: "The bigger the vision, the bigger the obstacle course." "You must create a vision and it must be uncomfortable." Sales, but where you are the product with networking as the conduit. The program itself, which is roughly two to three months, has flexible hours and the freedom to shop around for businesses that interest you. There's a ton of diversity in branch, rank, and time in service, and they have resources available to help you "find you," which I still argue is the most important part of the transition process.

I also kept working on my COMMIT modules to prepare for my third coaching session. Some really great stuff resonated with me, which came down to: "Do the damn thing." The video to open one of the lessons talked about confidence is built through successful repetition (e.g., interview practice), but at a certain point, you have to take the "Leap of Courage." Some people end up suffering from paralysis through analysis, and never actually make the jump. Or, worse, they are afraid of making that leap. As the presenter said, "Do the damn thing!" I ended up creating a visualization of what this looked like in my mind, and it forced me to reflect on the biggest thing I'm not doing: my résumé. I've had so much amazing help, and I have the tools, I just need to do it. And, as soon as I submit this entry, I'm doing it. I will do the damn thing, today, period.

ASKING FOR HELP

WHAT I'M READING AND LEARNING:
A few early mornings allowed me to get through some more of *Think Again*, and some nice long runs to clear my head allowed me to listen to *Robert E. Lee and Me*. Both books, while wildly different topics are challenging my thinking over and over again. I highly recommend both, and if you go in with an open mind to explore your own biases and entrenched thinking, you might find some great value in them.

SELF-REFLECTION(S) OF THE WEEK:
I suck at asking for help, and I am a serial-over committer. The workload came to a head this week, and I realized I have to ask for some relief from tasks to give me time to focus on the transition. I don't like that I have to step away from some things, as I feel like I'm not being a good teammate, but I have got to transition to take care of my family. I never see people asking me for help as a sign of weakness, but all too often I think I'll be perceived as weak if I need to take a step back. I cannot let that dominate my thinking, in particular when I absolutely need to put time into the transition to take care of my family. Fortunately for me, my boss was extremely understanding and supportive. We're going to work together to figure out a way ahead, and I'm very thankful for his willingness to support my transition.

DID I SUCCEED IN MY PREVIOUS GOAL(S):
I will! I was able to enjoy a nice weekend with the family, finished grading, and knocked out and reflected on the COMMIT modules. I haven't finished my taxes yet, but with my wife and kids visiting her sister for the weekend, I'm catching up on those tasks I have outstanding…and the fifteen chores to tidy up the house.

GOALS FOR NEXT WEEK:
Big teaching week, so I'm not pushing too hard next week for the transition (the following week is very transition focused). I have to prep some documents to do a will with Drew and the legal staff here at West Point, as well as wanting to have a really beneficial coaching session with Kyle, so I'm not committing to a lot to give me some flexibility.

INSPIRATION, PASSION, OR EXCITEMENT OF THE WEEK:
As part of the transition, I'm going to some appointments with my youngest daughter. She has iris coloboma (cat eye syndrome), and her optometrist said she needed to get glasses. While it is hard to assess if she can actually see better, the staff at her daycare said she was standing in front of the mirror smiling at herself! That made my heart so happy, and while we might not know if it's working for her, she looks adorable in them.

GRATITUDE:

Thanks to Tom Giboney and Russ Medina for providing me with some awesome advice for the transition and some specific info for the Dallas area. Thanks to Chris White and Jerrod Gaertner for introducing me to Sales Platoon, and Rod Hairston for his inspirational words. Finally, thanks to Russ Lemler for his leadership and care for me and my family. He is always willing to lend a hand with anything I need, and I can't thank him enough for his support during my transition.

IMPOSTER SYNDROME FIGHT:

So many people have invested in you, and you'll disappoint them when you fail.

REFLECTION QUESTION:
When you think about where your next career will take you: What support network is there? Who can you lean on? Who will you stay in touch with from your previous career to serve as a mentor?

Post 12:
THE FIRST TRY

Date: March 19, 2021

WHAT I DID THIS WEEK:

This was a big reset week, as I needed to put a lot of time into family endeavors, including my little brother visiting and meeting his new niece for the first time! It was awesome to surprise the kids with a visit from their uncle. I also had an incredible discussion about women in the military during a department meeting, as well as a chat with one of my former soldiers, Jonna. Brandon also facilitated my Friday classes, enabling my students to learn about leadership from a totally different lens. I'm so happy that he was able to make this happen, and I hope that my classes learned that the military approach is not always the best method.

Scott from USMA AOG also hit me up again and told me to start applying to positions…so I did! I made the first leap into throwing out my résumé, and I'm leveraging a series of contacts to see what I can dig up about the position. It is a very exciting role, and I'm curious how it will shake out! I also had my third coaching session with Kyle. One of the best pieces of reflection from that session was my "ideal day." Part of my prep was to build a detailed breakdown of my ideal day in Adventure 2.0 (post-transition). I put a lot of thought into what that day would look like (work out, make and have breakfast with the family, take kids to school, drive to work, etc.). The first thing that Kyle noticed threw me quite a bit…he noted that I made my ideal day a workday. I still haven't quite shaken that since we talked, as it made me realize that I've got a lot to unpack and unwind from my military service.

WHAT I'M READING AND LEARNING:

My department does a great job of using meetings to advance our culture (rather than just synchronizing information), and this week we did a Women's History Month trivia contest. I learned a ton about the women who fought oppression and broke glass ceilings to help improve the world. There are still so many gaps in my historical and cultural knowledge, and I'm also so excited to hear more powerful stories of people blazing the trail to fix issues.

SELF-REFLECTION(S) OF THE WEEK:

The COMMIT PYP modules and coaching prep really showed me that I desire some flexibility in my schedule to allow time for my family. I am realizing more and more how important this is to me, and it's helping me hone my potential employment opportunities for the future. Kyle helped me realize I need to start drawing on these ideas to neck down my options to those things that allow me to achieve balance in my personal and professional life.

DID I SUCCEED IN MY PREVIOUS GOAL(S):

Yes! Knocked them all out of the park, including refining and continuing to tweak my résumé. Granted, I didn't stretch too far this week in my goal setting, but I needed to put energy elsewhere.

GOALS FOR NEXT WEEK:

Allow the girls to enjoy their weekend with Uncle Luke! We're going to bust out the pizza oven tomorrow and maybe do s'mores outside. Should be a fun time for the kids to spend time with him before he heads back to Georgia. I also plan to contact VA claims to start the process, have an appointment for a will, SFL-TAP classes (need to finish all but one next week), and administer/grade a test. I have a lot of work to do on the transition classes that I've been pushing off, so I absolutely need to knock those out. I'll also tack in that I want to contact travel and housing to alert them to the move, just to add in some more goals! On top of all that, I have a really exciting conversation with someone inside of Korn Ferry, and I cannot wait to chat with them to learn more about the culture of the organization.

INSPIRATION, PASSION, OR EXCITEMENT OF THE WEEK:

Getting to catch up with Jonna was amazing. Hearing about her incredible life journey and where she's off to next was so inspiring. She's reflecting, writing, and doing incredible things in her industry, and I'm so proud of her!

GRATITUDE:

Thanks to Tom Giboney and Nick Cahill for shopping my résumé around. Tom, in particular, provided me with some great detailed feedback after sending it around to some other folks to help me refine the product some more. He also caught a rookie spelling error! Thanks to Kyle Moses for continuing to push me through coaching. Thanks to Scott for always keeping an eye out for me. Huge thanks to Brandon Walker for giving an incredible lecture and Q&A to my students. As of writing this, he spoke to my first-hour class, and he's going to talk to two more after lunch! Lastly, thanks to Jonna Eckenrod for staying in touch and sharing some of her professional writing with me. She's got some incredible things coming up, and I'm so excited and proud of her! She was a rockstar mechanic in my first unit, and she was hand-selected to join my platoon. She has since ventured out of the Army and has been doing amazing things, and it was awesome to catch up with her.

IMPOSTER SYNDROME FIGHT:

You'll never have the same quality of life as you do right now.

REFLECTION EXERCISE: ELEVATOR PITCH 0.9

Let's make a revision to your elevator pitch. Dust that thing off and read through it. You've done a lot since the last time you built it.

- What sticks out as an absolute keeper?

- What needs to get removed?

- Do you need to add anything new that you identified recently?

- How can you clarify it for your audience?

Go through and revise it with these posed questions to develop Version 0.9. Oh, and since I'm sure you're asking, why 0.9 and not 1? Or 2? In my brain, Version 1.0 is always the first time I feel comfortable sharing outside of my trusted circle. Maybe you're already there. But if I had to guess, probably not. That's okay! Even when I name documents, I don't put a "V1.0" on until I've shared it once with the intended audience. Then it goes into another pile of versioning control. I'm sure it doesn't make sense to you, but it does to me.

Wow, brains are weird, aren't they?

REFLECTION EXERCISE:
ELEVATOR PITCH V0.9

Positive opener and gratitude

Highlights
(use short reminder phrases)
1.

2.

3.

4.

Skills

1.
2.
3.
4.
5.
6.

Personal Story

The "Ask"

Gratitude!

Post 13:
LEADING WITH PURPOSE

Date: March 26, 2021

WHAT I DID THIS WEEK:
There was a lot of getting stuff done this week. Over the weekend, the girls got to play with Uncle Luke, which was an awesome time and a blast to see. He is the first member of my side of my family to be able to visit in more than a year due to the pandemic.

I also had a nice chat with Rob, who gave me some great advice and other things to research. I also had an awesome discussion with Mitali, and hearing about her experiences and role at Korn Ferry was amazing. In between finishing SFL-TAP (big step!). Drew and I also established a will. I met with Bob to talk about restructuring the rugby support program to make it more effective and run smoother after many of the mentors leave.

I also had a great opportunity to work with a group of cadets during an event called a "Leader's Challenge," which coincidentally included the story of one of my old company mates.

Walking cadets through these difficult scenarios really helps show them that character in leadership matters.

In that vein, I was selected for an interview as a role model for a former student as she navigates some difficult times following an honor violation. The ability to help someone deepen their reflection and growth following an issue is something I truly enjoy helping with, and it's always such a privilege to be selected.

Bob got me in touch with Todd, who walked a very similar path that I'm going down. After serving as a TAC and RXO, he left to pursue positions in Dallas in the leadership development space. Learning about his experiences was so much fun, and I look forward to staying in touch with him following the move.

I also got to participate in the USMA Combatting Extremism Stand-Down Day, and it provided me a great chance to reflect on how we can address issues within ourselves and our organization. We all struggle with finding the line between what is acceptable speech and where we move into dangerous territory, so having tough conversations was beneficial for all of us.

I was able to reconnect with Al, who is a family friend and a rugby fan. Every time we talk, he gives me another, extremely relatable, way to look at how my military experience can translate to value in the civilian world. One great example: creating a decision matrix to weigh your employment options. This was absolutely brilliant, and I put one together to help capture my values, the things that drain me, energize me, and some other factors. By weighting and scoring them, I can help somewhat objectify my employment opportunities. In addition, this helps me identify which questions I need to ask in interviews to answer key things that I don't know about to inform my decision-making. He also helped me talk through a ton of excellent interview questions to get at the difficult culture-related topics that help me learn about an organization while simultaneously demonstrating my potential value.

Thursday capped off with a memorable event where Yvette read her book about her father, MSG Roy Benavidez, to the team at S&P. I'm so thankful to be invited to these amazing events, and hearing *Tango Mike Mike* read by the author was inspiring. I finished up the week grading papers...whew!

WHAT I'M READING AND LEARNING:

Started *Leading from Purpose* (thanks, Al!), which has been an amazing book so far. Understanding the impact that having a clear purpose, and one that people can rally behind, in this increasingly complex world is invaluable and I'm very happy I've dedicated so much time to the endeavor. The more I hear from people about the importance of knowing your core values and purpose in life, the more I keep pushing that to others, and not just those going through a transition period!

SELF-REFLECTION(S) OF THE WEEK:

Leading from Purpose really got me thinking about my purpose, and while I'm holistically doing that through COMMIT and some other reflection, I took a stab at where I'm at right now. I need to refine it some more, which I expect to do over the next month or so. Here's the first draft:

My purpose in life is to improve others through my positive, engaged leadership. By demonstrating shared vulnerability, I strive to create psychologically safe environments to allow others to thrive. I work tirelessly to learn and grow every day, and I push others to do the same. I seek out the good in everything, trying to bring some fun into the day. My greatest joy comes from seeing others bloom into better versions of themselves and seeing them unlock more of their potential.

DID I SUCCEED IN MY PREVIOUS GOAL(S):

Yes! Holy cow, there were a lot of them and getting SFL-TAP is a huge weight off my shoulders. I've got so much more to do, but the pieces are starting to come together!

GOALS FOR NEXT WEEK:

First VA appointment, finish COMMIT modules, do a Podcast with Natasha, finish grading tests. I also need to put some time into the lodge website, which I will do by the end of next week.

INSPIRATION, PASSION, OR EXCITEMENT OF THE WEEK:

Seeing Luke with the girls was amazing. They loved playing with him and getting to catch up was a blast. Al gave me a great confidence boost in letting me know that I'm going down the right trail with how I'm approaching my transition. I still have so much more to do to make myself as competitive as possible, but his words of encouragement meant a lot.

GRATITUDE:

Thanks to Rob for reaching out and talking shop with me about leadership, as well as giving me some other stuff to add to the research queue. Thanks to Mitali for taking the time to chat with me, it was fun to learn about Organizational Strategy and her advice to find what speaks to me I will carry forward. Thanks to Bob for being a great advocate for the rugby team. I miss wandering the hallway to talk to "the oracle" when I was in my previous job, he helped me more than anyone else keep my sanity and my regiment afloat. Thanks to Tod for talking with me and helping me recant war stories from RXO life. Hearing about his journey showed me that I, too, can take my degree and follow my passions. Thanks to Adam for continuing to invite me to participate in incredible events with S&P. And finally, huge thanks to Al for his wisdom and for taking the time to talk with me. We first met at the Southgate Tavern after a rugby game, and he told me very specifically to reach out to him when I started my transition. He's kept in touch with me through the years, helping me make new connections, and his advice was invaluable and put my mind slightly at ease.

IMPOSTER SYNDROME FIGHT:

There's too much to do and not enough time to do it. You won't be ready in time.

REFLECTION QUESTION:

Who is there to pick you up if you fall?

Or

What was one of your "comeback" stories where you failed and came back better?

_____
_____
_____
_____
_____
_____
_____
_____
_____
_____
_____

Post 14:
FOLLOW THROUGH

Date: April 2, 2021

WHAT I DID THIS WEEK:

This week was focused on a lot of reflection and soul-searching. Whether reflecting on all of my previous injuries and current ailments for my VA medical paperwork, trying to apply my strengths in more deliberate ways via my COMMIT modules, or participating in an awesome coaching event put together by Rob with Jim from Untamed, it was a week of looking at myself in the mirror. Early in the week, one of my former cadets (now a first lieutenant—I'm getting old!) stayed with us as she did a recon of USMA for cadet summer training. It's crazy to think that my first batch of cadets is moving along in the Army…and that they will be captains soon! I also got to record a podcast with Natasha to talk about coaching and how I leverage the skillset in developing leaders. As an NCO she attended BLDP the first year I worked with the program, and two years later she was teaching Executive Coaching at BLDP! I love learning from her and her work ethic and thirst for knowledge is unlike anyone I've met. I am also working with Josh and his wife, Lindsey, to teach some leadership theories (Power, Full-Range Leadership, and Toxic Leadership) to leaders at Keller Army Community Hospital. He challenged me to change up my usual teaching method and content to be more engaging with the audience, and I'm very proud of how my material is shaping up, and I truly hope I'm able to help these critical leaders get better.

While it's all well and good to reflect on the past, I am pushing to the future simultaneously...Drew and I started talking with a relator in the Dallas area and are finding our next home! This is a huge, crazy step for us, and we're full of anxiety and excitement about what the future holds. I also broke down and got some custom-fitted suits to up my game for the corporate world! I'm finishing up this week with my fourth coaching session with Kyle and updating the lodge website with some more photos and details to engage more potential clients. It's going to be a busy Friday moving into the holiday weekend with the family!

WHAT I'M READING AND LEARNING:

I continue to work through *Leading from Purpose* and started the 20-minute networking meeting. I've been working on refining my brand and how I pitch myself more effectively in the condensed time that's impactful and respectful of people's time. I've done dozens of these meetings and reading that book earlier in my transition would have helped me be more effective in networking. I also refined my purpose in life further, moving away from a long, drawn-out purpose, to one more backed with a metaphor: *Inspiring home cooks to level up to chefs using the tools in their own kitchens.* *Leading from Purpose* helped me connect the child-like passions of sports/games and my love for cooking into something that speaks to me and hopefully others. I don't feel like it's perfect yet, but I like where I'm moving with it.

SELF-REFLECTION(S) OF THE WEEK:

I've been thinking a lot about purpose and passion recently and participating in the event led by Jim really helped me understand some of my human needs in a way that requires some additional unpacking. One big reflection I came to learn more about was a potential worry that I struggle with follow-through. I am a serial "80% and done" person, where I will learn something to the point of being pretty good, then move on to the next thing. Jim was able to help me realize that part of that is not being comfortable enough to take the step to mastery for fear of being found out as not good enough. He really helped me understand why I have this subconscious concern and helped me reframe it in a better way. Instead of trying to find the one thing you're the "8- or 9-out-of-10" at, find the bunch of "7s" and put those together in a unique way. I loved this approach and helped me find a healthier way to express the human need of uncertainty/variety that I can connect to my career ambitions and passions.

DID I SUCCEED IN MY PREVIOUS GOAL(S):

I did, and a whole lot more! Part of my COMMIT coaching work was to leverage my strengths in more deliberate ways. By leveraging my "arranger" skill to think through a more effective and efficient way to grade (and bonus help from my wife taking the kids to the store for a couple of hours), I was able to finish in record time! This made me want to be more mindful of how I approach my strengths to improve more.

GOALS FOR NEXT WEEK:

I'm going to dedicate next week to networking and make the goal of having five quality conversations. I have a light teaching week, so I also want to refine my lesson material through the rest of the semester. All of this is to set conditions for the following week, where I make the transition from learning to hunting (or for my military folks, from reconnaissance to the offensive).

INSPIRATION, PASSION, OR EXCITEMENT OF THE WEEK:

As part of the leadership course that I teach, we focus heavily on reflection. I try to take this a step further through my vulnerability to get my students to open up more about their struggles and experiences. This week, one of my students gave a presentation (I model the presentations after Next Jump's 10x with their radical feedback methods applied as well), and she blew the class away. Seeing her apply the course material, reflect openly, and share a deeply personal story that resonated and helped others learn was incredible. Her story and strength to share made me so proud and thankful for her leadership to her future soldiers!

GRATITUDE:

Thanks to Josh for bringing me into the fray to help teach at the hospital and continuing to motivate me to try new things. Thanks to Natasha for allowing me to ramble in a hopefully coherent way that provides value to her podcast. Thanks to Rob for putting together the event with Untamed, and thanks to TJ, Dan, Brent, Matt, and Rob for opening up and sharing their struggles with me so I could learn about them and myself. Finally, thanks to Jim for facilitating and providing me with the lens to view myself in a healthier way. I was in awe of his style and ability to engage a group and focus down to the individual in a way that helped everyone in the room learn. There were so many great nuggets I took away, but this spoke to me: "You have to meet your needs internally first, everything else is a bonus. But when those needs buckets are full, you can start to give to others."

IMPOSTER SYNDROME FIGHT:

You don't know enough people to make the next jump, nobody is going to help you.

REFLECTION QUESTION:

What about your current role do you love and want to continue in your next career?

Post 15:
NETWORKING, REDESIGNED

Date: April 9, 2021

WHAT I DID THIS WEEK:

After a great Easter weekend with the family (and my wife helping put together a fun little neighborhood Easter egg hunt), this was a busy, busy week. I was able to chat over the weekend with Rob for a bit about coaching as a profession, as I'm being drawn more and more to getting certified as an executive coach. He helped guide me on some certification ideas and assessments that he uses. I also got in touch with UT Dallas to see about doing their PCC program and, depending on how the job search turns out, I might try and hop into their August cohort. It seems like a great program, and I'm trying to line up a discussion with a graduate in the near future to learn more about their experience. I also had a great discussion with Kelly to learn more about Bain, and she gave me some amazing advice and other things to research. I also had a great chat and caught up with an old friend, Len, who works at Accenture. Learning about Kelly and Len's pathways and how far they've come was awesome and learning more about their experience in their organizations was enlightening for my job search.

I was able to learn more about Splunk from Brandon, a Marine Corps veteran with an incredible background. For my fellow transitioning veterans who are interested in pursuing IT/ Cyber pathways, please check out Splunk, as Brandon and the rest of the vets in the company are so incredible and willing to help out! Rob also got me in touch with Mark, who is operating in a really amazing leadership development space at GE (and his TED talk is awesome as well!). Getting to talk through leadership topics like the importance of followership was super fun and I look forward to staying in touch with him in the future.

On top of all of that, I took the opportunity to get ahead of the game on my course work for teaching, and I have the majority of my lessons prepped for the rest of the semester. The last two big tasks I'll have to complete for the year will be grading a paper (well, thirty-seven of them...) and a final, which is going to be tough with the time constraints, but it'll get done! Another awesome experience I had this week was doing my final coaching modules for "Pursue Your Purpose" with the COMMIT foundation. In addition to finishing the modules, I conducted some extra work from Kyle to help me visualize the next 5 years on my professional path. I've got some great ideas, so now the next step is to find the right fit for employment!

Last, one of the biggest discussions I had this week was with Rick, and I'm very thankful for his assistance. He helped Drew and me understand the VA loan process, and I learned that if you are leaving the military, you need to have proof of employment beyond your ETS date. This blindsided me, and with how chaotic the market is in DFW, Drew and I are now looking at renting. While initially disappointing, as we were so excited to own a home for the first time, we see it as a blessing in disguise. In renting, we can have a clearer understanding of our employment situation (location and pay scale), and then we can start to build our own home for a long-term solution. This alleviates a lot of problems with our transition to the area, and I think in the long run will be a great thing.

Oh, and in huge news, HRC approved my paperwork so I should have my orders early next week! This is massive, as it will allow me to start scheduling HHG shipping, turning in my equipment, and all the other random tasks I need to complete to clear the Army.

WHAT I'M READING AND LEARNING:

I continue to work through *Leading from Purpose* and finished the *20-Minute Networking Meeting*. I feel really good about my current purpose, so much so that I added it and my core values to my résumé. While unconventional, I feel it's important for an employer to know who I am and what's important to me. If that speaks to them, I believe the hiring process will go much smoother. Also, the author, Nick, reached out to me! I was freaking out, and it was fate that he did so when I had just finished the portion of the book where he talked about coming to West Point and working with Tony Burgess and COL Spain, my professors from one of my graduate school courses (and COL Spain is my current boss).

I also took a ton of notes from the *20MNM*, and in conjunction with Al's feedback from last week, I'm currently at 5 pages of notes about my elevator pitch, the twenty-minute meeting cheat sheet, and stories tied to my core values, strengths, weaknesses, and brief examples of accomplishments. By doing research about the organization, I'm networking (or interviewing) with, tailoring my stories to show examples of my qualifications or ways I can use my skills to help provide value for them, and being positive and gracious, I'm confident that I'll be improving my networking skills drastically!

SELF-REFLECTION(S) OF THE WEEK:

By pure, dumb luck, I've been doing a good job at networking so far. While I wish I had read the *20-Minute Networking Meeting* prior to starting my networking blitz, I was naturally doing well at the process. I have been exploring gratitude further (and incorporating it into the lessons I teach), I try to do my research and homework prior to talking to someone to maximize their time and help me ask better questions, and I am always very positive and want to learn about them and their experiences. Where I've been falling short is following up, which I'm going to do a much better job of in the future. I also need to refine some critical parts of my story to increase the brevity and impact.

DID I SUCCEED IN MY PREVIOUS GOAL(S):

Yes, I had five quality conversations! Tack on the discussion with my ACP mentor and talking with Rick, and finishing my lesson material for the semester, it was a big win! Another random thing I was able to knock out was building my "nudges" for the rest of the semester. I'm working with a professor in my department to test out Nudging via Qualtrics, in the hopes that I can improve my student's multiple-choice scores on their finals. Having that done is a load off my shoulders, and I hope it pays off for them and with data for my department!

GOALS FOR NEXT WEEK:

Huge teaching week, so light on the goals. I want to commit to two quality networking conversations and setting the stage for my clearing of the Army (schedule HHG, notify housing, schedule equipment turn-in, etc.).

INSPIRATION, PASSION, OR EXCITEMENT OF THE WEEK:

This one goes out to my wife, Drew. After the disappointment about not being able to purchase a home through the VA, she immediately pivoted to renting and got me really excited about finding a better home for us. It is so helpful to have a partner in this process, and I'm glad we're working as a team in this process. If anyone needs a woman veteran with experience in HR, an MBA, and a PMP certification, please hit her up!

GRATITUDE:

Thanks to Rob for getting me in touch with Mark and inspiring me to pursue coaching further. Thanks to Kelly for her words of wisdom and for providing me with some other great things to look into. Thanks to Len for taking time away from his new baby (congrats!) to chat with me and catch up. Thanks to Brandon and Mark for sharing their journey with me and answering my questions. Thanks to Kyle for continuing to challenge me via coaching. Big thanks to my wife for her continued support in this difficult process. Thanks to Nick Craig, Dr. Marcia Ballinger, and Nathan Perez for their amazing books that have helped me so much along my journey. And last, thanks to Rick for his assistance. I was extremely disappointed with the news about the VA loan, but he fought to help me understand the process and gave me a better way to think about the future. I'm going to take his advice and move forward so we can set ourselves up better for the next opportunity!

IMPOSTER SYNDROME FIGHT:

Why can't you accomplish your goals, what's wrong with you?

REFLECTION EXERCISE: THE VENN DIAGRAM OF CAREER SATISFACTION

As mentioned in the post, I found incredible value in Tim's statement to find the intersection of "What do I bring to the table, the demand in the market, and which industries interest me?" Let's take that a bit further.

I'm going to have to dig up the previous work you've done, as well as dig into some more things. Our goal is to identify positions that live in the nexus of your Venn Diagram. However, I want to caution you, it probably won't be perfect. That's okay! There are other ways to get to that nexus; it might just take a while. I also started to identify potential "watch outs" if you only find yourself in overlaps between two of the three circles.

If you find a position that aligns with your skills and interests, but not market demand, there's a possibility of low, or niche, positions. You can overcome this with aggressive, strategic networking, which we'll get into in another exercise.

Similarly, if you align your skills and the market demand, but not your interest, there's a chance you won't be satisfied. That's all right! Maybe you find your energy outside of work so this isn't a big problem for you. Also, this could simply be a jumping-off point for you, the classic "suck it up for a few years" idea then catapult to another more satisfying job.

Last, if you find something that is in high demand and interests you, but you don't have the skills, there's a chance you will have a low application success rate. We can overcome that by looking back on our Needs Survey and finding something that can bolster your résumé by adding a credential or certification that's valuable.

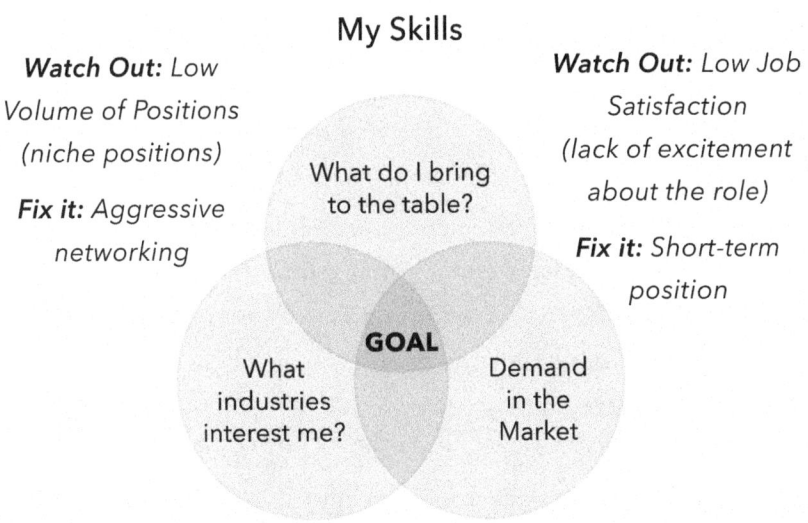

Let's start by reflecting and flesh out your KSAOs to help us determine what you bring to the table, thanks to the lovely folks at Gartner (https://www.gartner.com/en/human-resources/glossary/knowledge-skills-abilities-and-other-characteristics-ksaos-):

- Knowledge: "the body of factual or procedural information that can be applied, such as knowledge of foreign languages or computer programming languages"

- Skills: "the capabilities require to perform tasks accurately, such as psychomotor activities like typing speed or driving ability"

- Abilities: "more stable characteristics that can include cognitive, sensory and physical abilities, such as empathy"

- Other Characteristics: "values, work style, personality and degrees, and certifications"

You've already started looking into this with previous exercises, but let's think through what industries interest you. Are you a school-trained civil engineer and want to get into that world? Do you love human resources? Reflect, using your prior work from this book, to identify more things you're interested in.

Finally, let's take a look at the market demand. This one is a bit tricky, as it can depend on your location. But for this exercise, do your best to keep it broad, as the discussion about location will come later.

If you haven't identified a common theme yet, guess what? It's time to start…researching…again. Check out resources such as *Fast Company*, *McKinsey Insights*, or dig into LinkedIn and snoop around. Are there some hot things coming up? Cyber is all the rage right now, for example. Similarly, see if you can find some dying industries.

- Are there things that just don't look good for the future?

- What are some "hot" industries?

- What are some "dying" industries?

With that additional context, start checking those "hot" industry job boards and find some things that are generally aligned with your KSAOs and Interests. But keep an open mind because there might not be a perfect fit just yet. But you never know, you'd be surprised what might shake out of the tree!

REFLECTION EXERCISE:
THE VENN DIAGRAM OF CAREER SATISFACTION

KSAOs	Hot	Dying

My Skills

My Interests

What's Needed

What excites me?

Post 16:
LEARNING AND TEACHING

Date: April 16, 2021

WHAT I DID THIS WEEK:

After a great chat last Friday with Neil, my ACP mentor, I jumped into the weekend with both feet on a mission to learn more about *ghSMART*. Following a discussion with Kelly, she mentioned them, and I took note and investigated their website. I was immediately drawn to their credo, values, and the incredible people within the organization. I realized they had a few books published focusing on their work and findings, and I ended up reading all of them over the next three days. There were some incredible lessons about hiring the right people (*Who: The A Method for Hiring*), having the right Priorities, Who, and Relationships (*Power Score: Your Formula for Leadership Success*), and ways to develop into or select a great CEO (*The CEO Next Door*). Learning more about the incredible work this organization has done and continues to do, coupled with its culture, made me reach out to them. They were so helpful and scheduled an initial phone discussion. Getting to learn more about Sydney and what the company does was amazing, but unfortunately, I was not selected as a candidate to move forward in the interview process. I was pretty bummed, but I look forward to staying in touch, and maybe down the road I might be a more viable candidate!

Aside from personal endeavors, I had an extremely busy teaching week, coupled with a ton of individual mentorship for some of my cadets. Through all this, I also was lucky enough to get to work with the Keller Army Community Hospital to teach lessons on leadership to more than 40 of their leaders (both civilian and military). Being able to engage with a passionate group that works so hard in demanding roles was so incredible, and I hope they took away some techniques to help level up their game! I also was fortunate enough to be selected to teach a lesson on Assessing Organizational Culture with…Indra Nooyi!!! Having her observe my class, then provide some incredible wisdom from her amazing career was truly awe-inspiring. I remember studying her as she took over PepsiCo when I was a cadet. Seeing what she did with the company and where she's gone since is a case study of how leaders can directly influence the trajectory of organizations through transformational leadership and a compelling vision.

In between all of this, I was able to talk to Pat about franchise ownership, as well as catch up with Chad on his transition journey. Oh, and I finally talked with the VA and scheduled the first four of my nine medical appointments. Frustratingly, the *closest* one is in the Bronx, one is on Broadway (at 9 a.m.…which is going to be a joy to get to), and one is more than two hours away in Connecticut! I'm not sure why these appointments are so far away, but I've got to do what I've got to do!

WHAT I'M READING AND LEARNING:
As mentioned, Who, *Power Score*, and *The CEO Next Door* taught me some powerful lessons about leadership and how important selecting the right people is to an organization's success. There have been very few opportunities in my career to "pick my team," so it was enlightening to read about an organization that focuses so heavily on a process to make those decisions. It felt foreign, but also familiar, and I hope to someday engage in the hiring process and use their techniques!

SELF-REFLECTION(S) OF THE WEEK:
I'm reaching a weird stage of the transition where I worry about being underqualified. I assume this is partly imposter syndrome, but to this point, I have failed to acquire tangible certifications or "hard skills" that are easy to translate into industries I'm excited about. I slide back and forth on this scale of "My experience and education are adequate" to "You've wasted your time and need to go back to get an MBA and XYZ certification." I'm going to get certified in agile techniques through O2O, and I'm continuing to look into professional coaching certification programs and MBAs, but I'm worried I'm too late to the party.

DID I SUCCEED IN MY PREVIOUS GOAL(S):

My orders didn't come through yet, so I did not schedule the things I wanted to. I did succeed in having some great conversations, though, and I scheduled a bunch of medical appointments!

GOALS FOR NEXT WEEK:

Another light week on goals, as I'll be commuting for three different medical appointments. That ten-ish hours on the road (or train) will give me ample time to read, so I'll shoot to finish a couple of books over the next week. I'm also attending a PCC info session for UT Dallas and an Organizational Change presentation put on by a couple of my professors from grad school. Assuming my orders actually come in, I'll also schedule my out-processing tasks.

INSPIRATION, PASSION, OR EXCITEMENT OF THE WEEK:

This is a very small one, but it made me very happy on a personal level. One of my upcoming classes is a "class selected topic." I change these up every semester, and I typically either do a case study or let the students select something (or invite a guest speaker). This semester, I had them vote on a series of options, one of them is to "drop" the class, so we would have a day off. I've had students vote on this in previous semesters, and every time the class has almost universally voted to have the class off. This semester, across all my students, only three wanted to *not* come to class. I was not expecting that they actually wanted to come to class in lieu of not...

and I actually felt like I was making headway on them caring about the material. I even heard one of them say as they left: "I've never had a class where people actually voted to stay in class." That made me feel really good...small victories!

GRATITUDE:

Thanks to Dave at Korn Ferry for helping mentor me through the transition process and making connections for me within the company. Thanks to Neil for his wisdom last week. Thanks to Sydney for taking the time to talk with me and learn more about me and share her experience with *ghSMART*. Thanks to Chad for helping keep me motivated during this tough process. Thanks to Pat for taking the time to talk with me so I could learn more about his journey, I look forward to learning more! Thanks again to Josh and Lindsey for the honor to help teach the Keller Team. Lastly, thanks to Indra for her wisdom in my class and for making me elevate my game on a Friday morning!

IMPOSTER SYNDROME FIGHT:

What if you can't find a new career? What will you do?

REFLECTION QUESTION:

From the perspective of your personal life, what do you want to continue in your next adventure?

Post 17:
YOU CAN'T BE WEAK

Date: April 23, 2021

WHAT I DID THIS WEEK:
Let's start a bit differently this week. Something resonated with me while I listened to the *Power of Vulnerability* from Dr. Brown. She mentioned how in her upbringing, she was socialized to believe that being sick, taking time off, or slowing down was unacceptable. I realized that I was raised the same way, both at home and in the Army. I set horrible examples for my subordinates as I almost never took leave, and even those times when I was on leave, I would still work. Even while in route to West Point, with 30 days to relax after my previous assignment, I found a way to teach a class on defensive operations at Oklahoma University's ROTC program. The last time I took leave was more than a year ago when I spent the majority of the time at an indoor water park on the phone/computer listening to briefings for work about how we were going to respond to the pandemic. It is a problem, and it comes back to something that Dr. Brown mentioned: You can't be weak.

While driving to my first VA appointment in South Manhattan in NYC rush hour traffic, I realized that this was insanity. I was scheduling appointments in between my teaching days, while trying to network and apply to jobs, find a house, prepare a move, find schools, all to leave the Army and start working another job within a couple of weeks. I decided, after talking with my wife, that I'm taking time off. I'm going to take two months to settle the family, relax, and figure out who I am post-transition. I've got some things I'll be working on (Agile Certification, applying to be a certified coach, etc.), but I want to be able to focus on my kids, my wife, and myself. I'm tired of thinking that taking time off is weak. With all of that out in the open, I'm dialing back the intensity of my transition and it feels like a tremendous weight lifted off my shoulders. I can put more time into enjoying my last bit of time at West Point rather than holed up in my office constantly checking LinkedIn for updates. I'm ready to enjoy the next steps.

Okay, so back to the regularly scheduled program. After getting my orders on Friday, I started work on the clearing processes. I'm working the HHG move, did the bulk of my Phase-One medical appointments (after canceling my VA appointments until I get to Texas); inventoried and cleaned my gear to prep for turn-in; and still had some time to do some awesome stuff. I was able to attend a Change presentation by Dr. Stilwell, one of my professors from Columbia, and Aimee and Daniel were there as well! It was awesome to see some familiar faces. I also lucked out and met Jacquie, a fellow BS&L alumnus who taught

"Psychology for Leaders" and was a grad of the same program at Teachers College. I'm so excited to learn about her career path following teaching and where she's ended up! I also had a chance to reconnect with Dr. Pasmore, another former professor of mine, who came armed to help me out. It felt like he had his Rolodex in hand as he doled out incredible resources to assist me in the transition. He also confirmed my decision to take time off and to attack the professional coaching certification. He also gave me awesome advice on which assessment to pursue first.

As I do more research about venturing out on my own, I also talked with Pat quite a bit about franchise coaching opportunities, and also attended a UT Dallas info session for their PCC program. Regardless of the next steps, I plan on applying for and starting their classes in August. I'm exploring which assessments I should get certified in, as there are so many I've used in the past. I've received some great advice and I'm starting to narrow down which ones I want to leverage in the future.

In the teaching world, after having Indra join my class last Friday morning, I took my afternoon classes on cultural "Walking Tours" to identify artifacts (in line with Schein's Iceberg) around the academy. As we walked around, we actually bumped into the Superintendent, LTG Williams, and he spent about 20 minutes helping me teach (his MA is in organizational psychology as well). This was totally unexpected but an awesome experience!

Not to be outdone (that day was hard to top), I had the honor of U.S. Rep. Steve Womack joining my class Friday morning as we talked about "Socialization" (aka onboarding). His advice to the cadets was extremely helpful and it was a blast to have him join us. Learning about his experiences with Socialization and how frequently members of the House experience the process was very eye-opening.

WHAT I'M READING AND LEARNING:

I mentioned quite a bit about what I've taken from Brené Brown's book *The Power of Vulnerability,* but I also started my Agile Certified Practitioner course through Onward 2 Opportunity (O2O). Learning about the Agile methodologies was a total shift in my headspace and I'm excited to continue the program.

SELF-REFLECTION(S) OF THE WEEK:

I hit on this up front, but I'll reiterate: taking time off is not a weakness. I have to break this habit. To give another level of how bad this was for me: the pandemic allowed me to bank extra leave days (usually our max is 60 before we start to lose them). *I have 113 days of leave before my transition.* Obviously, that's awesome, but what it says is that I haven't taken substantial time off in a very, very long time.

DID I SUCCEED IN MY PREVIOUS GOAL(S):

Well, I canceled the rest of my VA appointments, and thus shifted priorities around. I did quite a few out-processing tasks but did not finish any books. I did, however, put that time into the O2O

Agile course, which I plan to chip away at for the next couple of months. Overall, I did not succeed in my goals, but I'm not upset with myself as the priorities changed mid-week.

GOALS FOR NEXT WEEK:

I've got some great networking discussions lined up, as well as my last coaching session, but my biggest focus is grading. The last paper my students turn in is ready for grading, so I have 37 papers to go through. I have the goal to complete them by Friday (the 30th) so I can put my heart into my last week of teaching. The last lesson, "In Extremis Leadership," is by far my favorite class to teach and I go all out for it, so I'd like to put every bit of my energy into that.

INSPIRATION, PASSION, OR EXCITEMENT OF THE WEEK:

It's easy to feel the crushing weight of this change, whether through declined job applications, countless hours of effort, or the stress of losing a steady paycheck (and benefits). But I'm continually inspired by people willing to give their time and energy to provide advice. One great example among many is my former professors from Teachers College. This week alone, despite their enormous workload, three of them spoke to me about the transition in various forms. Their support is just awesome and gives me a boost of energy just thinking about it!

GRATITUDE:

Thanks to Dr. Stilwell for the awesome class, as well as thanks to Aimee, Daniel, and Jacquie for joining me in the experience! Thanks to Trish for reaching out and setting up a call with me, I'm stoked to learn more about her journey. Thanks to LTG Williams for joining my class. Thanks to Dr. Buontempo for her continued support of me and the USMA relationship. She's an absolute rockstar and it's always a joy to get to talk to her, even if it's by email. Thanks to Pat for providing me with a ton of information to learn more about future opportunities. Thanks to Rep. Womack for joining the class with us. Massive thanks to Dr. Pasmore for talking with me about the next steps. After a pretty tough week, having him come to the plate with his experience, contacts, and advice was so reassuring that there's a powerful network of people willing to give their time and energy to assist those in need of a helping hand.

Overall, I don't think I say enough thanks to those who spend their time and energy talking with me. For context, I'm at 53 conversations that have generated an MS Word Document with notes. The fact that 50+ people have taken the time to talk with me is so incredibly humbling and I'm so lucky to have them in my life.

IMPOSTER SYNDROME FIGHT:

Your weakness will make you fail, and everyone depends on you.

REFLECTION QUESTION:

How do you plan to say connected with your friends?

_____
_____
_____
_____
_____
_____
_____
_____
_____
_____

Post 18:
ONE MORE MONTH

Date: April 30, 2021

WHAT I DID THIS WEEK:

Another wild week full of a ton of great conversations with some amazing people, and now I'm within a month from leaving West Point and starting terminal leave...

On Friday, I had the chance to talk with Doug, a USMA grad who is passionate about coaching. Learning about his background and experiences following leaving the Army was super fun and it was a blast to talk coaching with him. I also finished up the COMMIT Foundation's Pursue Your Purpose after my fifth and final coaching session with Kyle. I cannot recommend COMMIT highly enough. If you're trying to figure out who you are and what you want, it is a powerful tool if you're willing to do the work. I also had an awesome conversation with Jacquie, whom I met last week during a webinar. Her perspective as someone who comes from the same educational and professional background, coupled with leaving the Army at the same time, and even ending up in an industry I want to join soon was so amazing. I also had the chance to talk with Trish, who gave me so many amazing contacts and talked me through the work she does at Leadership Worth Following and the DRiV assessment. She's been connecting me with great people and I'm so grateful to have met her! After talking with Trish, I was able to connect with Don, who recently joined Slalom and he explained to me what it's like to onboard there. They sound like an incredibly veteran-friendly organization that has a great culture, so be sure to check them out!

Wow, that's just through Monday. Tuesday, I had the chance to talk branch mentorship with one of my students, reconnect with my classmate and buddy Charles who gave me some other amazing things to look into, talked with Danny about licensing the Catalyft Coaching Model, and finished up the day talking with Mark McKearn. He is an executive coach and was my former Brigade Tactical Officer, and he's an amazing person and was so kind to talk with me for over an hour about the industry. Wednesday was another fun day (after the COVID test, that is...), where I had Matt, Ken, and Ben join my classes as guest facilitators and speakers. In between teaching I also had the absolute pleasure to do a *20-Minute Networking Meeting* with Nathan...who literally wrote the book on it (like...seriously...the author). Getting to learn more about his background, work, and passion for supporting the veteran community was so fun. My hope is that I passed what I can only describe as the final test for networking! I also had my final rater evaluation counseling with COL Woodruff, and he gave me a lot of other great things to think through with my transition.

Thursday things finally calmed down a bit as I took care of some transition tasks such as cleaning the rest of my gear, but I met with Sheri and Jackie to talk through franchising opportunities for coaching firms. I also snuck in an evening call with Ellen to talk through Slalom some more. They are such an interesting company, and I was super excited to learn more. I finished out the week with a nice check-in with Pat.

Disappointingly, I was slated to work the sideline tonight for the last rugby match this season, which was sadly canceled. I'll be spending the afternoon with the team, and who knows what sorts of shenanigans we will get into…Oh, my little brother got promoted to captain today as well!

WHAT I'M READING AND LEARNING:

I spent a lot of time listening to others share their experiences leading and coaching from different contexts. I also read "The Search for Worthy Leadership," which was a great article. I was on the move quite a bit today, so I spent a lot of time listening to podcasts, but nothing directly tied to the transition (which is perfectly fine by me!).

SELF-REFLECTION(S) OF THE WEEK:

Every conversation I've had, the things I've read, and the things I care about keep pushing me toward the importance of character. I want to be able to apply my desire to help people improve their character through leadership in the future. What that looks like is the great mystery…

DID I SUCCEED IN MY PREVIOUS GOAL(S):

Yes! My wife took the kids shopping and let me grade early in the morning so I could free up some time to finish early in the week. This took so much stress off of me to focus on networking and preparing for later lessons.

GOALS FOR NEXT WEEK:

Drew's parents come in this weekend, so I really want to spend some quality time with them. I also have some other important goals: finish my last two lessons of teaching at West Point with the energy to send off my students with some last good bits of knowledge. Help the rugby team with a staff org redesign. Provide my students with great feedback to improve their growth. Follow-on discussions about coaching licensing and franchising. Attend the SACC to continue to network.

INSPIRATION, PASSION, OR THE EXCITEMENT OF THE WEEK:

I cannot name them all, because at the end of this week I will have had 15 different networking discussions, which left me so inspired by their willingness to help. But what I keep coming back to is the notes from my guest speakers in class, but in particular what CSM Killingsworth told my students: "Are you trying to be the best platoon leader, or lead the best platoon?" This was such a powerful way to pull apart the individual from the team mindset and show my students how your focus should be on the organization and not yourself. That simplified term encapsulates what I've tried to teach over the last year, and it was so great of him to share.

GRATITUDE:

This is a big one! Thanks to Doug for the amazing talk, I look forward to staying engaged with him in the future. Thanks to Jacquie, Trish, Don, Charles, Mark, Nathan, and Ellen for taking time to talk with me and sharing your network. Thanks to Danny, Sheri, and Jackie for talking to me about running my own coaching business. Thanks to Matt, Ken, and Ben for helping me in the classroom and sharing your wisdom with my students. Thanks to Natasha for keeping her eyes peeled out there for me. Last, huge thanks to Kyle for his coaching. Not only did he help me out so much, but he also shared with me some additional wisdom about serving as a coach in the future. Thanks, everyone!

IMPOSTER SYNDROME FIGHT:

There are way too many people to talk to, and why would they waste their time with you anyway?

REFLECTION EXERCISE: THE DECISION-MAKING TRICYCLE

At this point, you have reflected on what career satisfaction looks like for you by assessing the intersection of your KSAOs, interests, and market demand. Let's take that a step further to help clarify some things for a huge decision.

Rob Stanton helped me think of the transition like a tricycle. For those who haven't ridden one in a while, the handle and peddles are connected to the front, large wheel. The rear two wheels are just along for the ride. In this metaphorical context, the big wheel is driving three of your biggest decisions: Where do you want to go, do, and how much do you want to make? The big wheel is entirely dictated by your personality and situation. It is also important to factor in your family dynamics and considerations. Let's explore by doing a totally unscientific calculation:

1. Where do you want to go?

    a) Is there a family requirement? Do you need to be close to family? Do you need to be far away from them?

    b) Do you want to live in a specific area? City? Region? Does that matter at all?

    c) When you're not working, what are your passions? Do you love the outdoors? Hunting? Mountains? Beaches? Travel? Do you want to be close to a major airport?

    Rate on a scale from 0: Not important to 5: Extremely important

2. What do you want to do?

   a) Do you have a very specific industry you are passionate about?

   b) Is there a specific company that you want to work for?

   c) Are you able to do what you want anywhere? Are there remote opportunities?

   d) Do you have a specific degree and/or skillset that you want to apply?

   Rate on a scale from 0: Not important to 5: Extremely important

3. How much money do you want to make?

   a) Is financial stability critical to you?

   b) Do you need rapid advancement?

   c) How much flexibility do you need in your work schedule?

   d) Will your spouse/partner/significant other be working as well?

   Rate on a scale from 0: Not important to 5: Extremely important

Make sure you talk this through with your family. If you want to make a ton of money, this will dictate many of your next steps. Do you want to be able to surf on the weekends? Again, this will help narrow down locations, and thusly job opportunities. Take time to think through and brainstorm with your family to help you figure out the driving wheel in your tricycle. Don't be afraid to ask them to rate these three things on the scale to see where the biggest differences are and talk. Then make the big decision and start peddling!

> **REFLECTION EXERCISE:**
> **THE DECISION-MAKING TRICYCLE**
>
> Where do you want to go? (Location)
>
> | 1 | 2 | 3 | 4 | 5 |
> |---|---|---|---|---|
> | Not Important | | | | Extremely Important |
>
> What do you want to do? (Job/Role)
>
> | 1 | 2 | 3 | 4 | 5 |
> |---|---|---|---|---|
> | Not Important | | | | Extremely Important |
>
> How much money do you want to make? (Money/Income)
>
> | 1 | 2 | 3 | 4 | 5 |
> |---|---|---|---|---|
> | Not Important | | | | Extremely Important |
>
> | Your High Score | Family High Score |
> |---|---|
> | Location | Location |
> | Job/Role | Job/Role |
> | Money/Income | Money/Income |
>
> What is your "Big Wheel?"

Post 19:
THE FINAL CLASS

Date: May 7, 2021

WHAT I DID THIS WEEK:

This was a tough week filled with some amazing conversations and events. Most importantly from a professional standpoint, I taught the last two lessons of my career at West Point. Closing up my room after my last student left was definitely a sad moment, but it was an absolute blast to get to do what I've done for the last year. Aside from that, this week I got to work with the coaching staff on the rugby team to help restructure the official representatives in a way that I hope will create some more predictability for all parties. Working with the team has been one of the highlights of my time here, and I hope to leave them in a better place. I also had the opportunity to do some one-on-one work with students to provide them performance-related feedback, and we were able to talk about some additional ways that I can improve and talk some extra "Army stuff" if they had questions. Those conversations are a blast and I hope to figure out a way to maintain a connection to the academy after I leave.

On the discussion side, I had the chance to meet with Kayla at TTI to learn about their available assessments, and I made a great connection with Harris at OKA. We actually had some mutual baseball friends from when he played at Lehigh! I also had some killer conversations with Tyler from McKinsey and Will at Pepsi, both of whom are crushing it in their position and provided me with some great insights about what it is to work at those companies. Following up on previous meetings, I met with Sheri and Danny to talk more about independent coaching options. I also had the great pleasure to talk with Dale and Myranda (the CEO and President) from Leadership Worth Following to learn more about their incredible organization.

I'm finishing up the week by attending the Service Academy Career Conference, but in classic over-commitment fashion, I have four calls scheduled during the event. I'm extremely excited to have these discussions and can't wait to learn more about the people and organizations I'm meeting with.

With all of that said, we overcame one of the biggest hurdles of the transition…we got a house! We did not realize how difficult it would be to buy a home, and we feel so fortunate to get something locked in and we're so excited!!!

WHAT I'M READING AND LEARNING:

Definitely a light week and I did not get much reading done. Much of my specific learning this week centered around the people and organizations I've had the opportunity to connect with.

THE FINAL CLASS

SELF-REFLECTION(S) OF THE WEEK:
Teaching, or facilitating a group event, is something that I'm realizing more and more gives me energy. I've done so many training sessions as an officer throughout my career, but I don't think I connected the dots between how much I enjoyed it in the past to how that influenced my love for my current role.

DID I SUCCEED IN MY PREVIOUS GOAL(S):
I did; however, I don't think I pushed myself hard (and that's okay by me!). Spending time with Drew's parents and getting to cook a whole bunch of good food (bringing mojo pork and about to start making Cuban bread as I write this) and finishing strong in the classroom was more important than pushing myself too hard on the transition side.

GOALS FOR NEXT WEEK:
Some more big transition events on the horizon, the scariest of which is...CIF turn-in. I have six bags and a tuff box™ of gear to turn in sitting in my garage right now, and I hope I cleaned it well enough! I also have a bunch of calls lined up, two finals to administer (and grade), as well as the farewell event for my department. It's going to be a busy week, so I'm only committing to knocking out the stuff I already have on my calendar!

INSPIRATION, PASSION, OR THE EXCITEMENT OF THE WEEK:

As part of my class, I give my students a "Leader Journal," which is the typical Army green notebook. I have them write a reflection from every lesson, usually tailored to the lesson and their role in the military. In my final class, I have them fill in a collaborative PowerPoint with their leadership tenets, and three key things from their leader journal. Seeing that learning and development come together at once is such a fun experience and something that always inspires me.

GRATITUDE:

This is a big one! Thanks to Kayla and Harris for talking with me about assessments. Thanks to the men's rugby team for letting me be a part of the program and pitch my idea for org redesign to better support the team going forward. Thanks to Danny and Sheri for our continued discussions. Thanks to Tyler and Will for the awesome talk and advice going forward, you both motivated me. Thanks to Dale and Myranda for taking the time to talk with me. Their focus on character and the vision of LWF is truly inspiring. Thanks to Edith our realtor for helping us find a house. Last, and most important this week, thanks to my students. I've held some amazing positions while serving in the Army, and many of them have different feelings (platoon leader was the most fun, the commander was the most impactful, and TAC was the most rewarding). Serving as a military leadership instructor helped me feel all those things at the same time, and it is because of my students who make it fun and go on the adventure with me!

IMPOSTER SYNDROME FIGHT:
It's getting pretty close to you leaving, you don't have enough time to get everything done.

REFLECTION QUESTION:
What are the three most exciting things about your next steps?

Post 20:
SMALL STEPS FORWARD

Date: May 14, 2021

WHAT I DID THIS WEEK:

After an incredible Friday talking with Dave, Mike, and Brian, all of whom are rock stars in their fields, I enjoyed the weekend with my wife's parents, and we made some great meals to celebrate their time here. Cuban sandwiches inspired by the film *Chef* and pizza from the outdoor oven were some high points! In addition to that, the episode of Natasha's podcast we recorded together dropped, and it was so fun to review our conversation.

After saying goodbye to the family, this was a slower week as I did a lot of small tasks to get me to the finish line. Between getting the utilities set up for the move and doing research about the new area, we're beyond excited to launch into our new lives. I also cleared some bigger hurdles, such as my final physical exam and I cleared CIF as a first-time go! Dropping off all of my gear collected over 12 years felt odd, but also very satisfying as the back of the SUV went from stuffed full to one box remaining.

This week also marked my last interactions with my students via our final exam. Being able to give them one last fist bump and wish them well was awesome but came with a twinge of sadness. This was a great group of students and I'm truly excited to see them excel in the future. In between prepping for the exam and grading, I was able to chat with Michel and Steena, two incredible leaders in their organizations. I also got to meet Julian, who built his own community in the OD space in NYC. I also had a really amazing call with Jan, and he gave me some incredible advice about entrepreneurship that I needed to hear. I also had a great call with Lauren on Thursday to learn more about Korn Ferry and we were able to share in our struggle as parents of young children during the pandemic. I even had the chance to catch up with Brandon to see how his journey has progressed, it had been a bit since we talked, and it was a blast to learn about the big steps he's taken in his life! Friday morning, I had the opportunity to attend the Core Leadership Institute Introductory Session after an invite from Nick Craig, which included incredible people from across the globe. Hearing stories and purpose statements from leaders from France, Singapore, and India was so inspiring. Hearing Jonathan share his story resonated deeply with me and was truly inspiring.

After publishing today, I have an assessment debrief session with Harris this afternoon and administering my final...final... ever. Capping off a busy week will be my department farewell, where my family and I will get to formally say goodbye to the Department of Behavioral Sciences and Leadership. It's going to be a sad but fulfilling day.

WHAT I'M READING AND LEARNING:
Thirty-seven finals were quite a bit of reading! I think a crucial thing I learned this week unrelated to the rest of my adventures came from Adam Grant's podcast, where he talked about pay transparency. This speaks in large part to my core value of justice, and it was great to hear someone in the field I respect deeply tackle a tough subject (and one that seems to be extremely relevant as we as a society return to normal).

SELF-REFLECTION(S) OF THE WEEK:
I'm really going to miss teaching, and I feel like a made a strong impact on this group of cadets. I put my heart into this last semester to "leave it on the floor," and I hope they took some good lessons away!

DID I SUCCEED IN MY PREVIOUS GOAL(S):
Absolutely!

GOALS FOR NEXT WEEK:
Clear, clear, clear. Also enjoy our last full week of time at West Point, which will be peppered with the rugby farewell banquet, my mom coming into town, McKinley's dance recital, and MEAT FEST 2021 with my boss, LTC Lemler! I want to be in the moment next week, so I'm keeping the goals light.

INSPIRATION, PASSION, OR EXCITEMENT OF THE WEEK:

My boss, COL Spain, taught me so much about gratitude, and getting to write 37 thank-you notes to my students was very exciting. Seeing the look on their faces as I handed out the notes after they turn in their last test was awesome, and I hope they enjoyed the personalized letter.

GRATITUDE:

Thanks to Dave for spending time talking with me about his experiences. Thanks to Mike for sharing his journey with ILEC. Thanks to Brian for helping me understand using Better Up to hone my searches. Thanks to Natasha for letting me join her and ramble for 30 minutes! Thanks to Michel for taking time out of his busy schedule to talk with me about Leadership Development at Korn Ferry. Thanks to Steena for chatting with me about FMI and her awesome experiences in Tanzania! Thanks to Julian for sharing his massive network and his passion for OD and community building. Thanks to Jan for giving me some candid, tough love about the importance of sales. Thanks to Lauren for sharing more about Korn Ferry and commiserating with me. Thanks to Brandon for catching up with me and being a positive light in my journey. Thanks to Nick for reaching out to let me sit in on the CLI intro session, and the team at CLI for facilitating an awesome webinar, in particular Jonathan. Thanks to Adam Grant for just being damn awesome. Thanks to my boss, LTC Lemler, for his support during my transition and putting together a great event to say goodbye.

Thanks to COL Spain for teaching me about gratitude. And last, thanks to Matt and Janet for stopping by to help us with the kiddos and eat tasty foods!

IMPOSTER SYNDROME FIGHT:
Something is going to go wrong. It always does.

REFLECTION QUESTION:
How do you relax? What recharges your batteries?

Post 21:
NOT GOODBYE, SEE YOU SOON

Date: May 21, 2021

WHAT I DID THIS WEEK:
Last Friday was a tough but fun day. After meeting with Harris to discuss my DRiV and EQi 260 results, I proctored my final…final. I had some time to sneak away to the ELDP graduation to see the next crop of fresh-faced TACs and catch up with my TC professors. It was so awesome to see some stellar leaders walking across the stage, and to see David in particular, who was a rock star lieutenant I served with a few years back.

I went from there to grab the family and headed to our Department farewell event, where I was officially sent off with an amazing little ceremony. It was truly a sad day and I'm so thankful to have been part of the BS&L team here at West Point. So many remarkable leaders have helped me along the way, and I'm so thankful for my time serving in this organization. In his special way, COL Spain made everyone feel good about saying farewell by saying: "This is not goodbye; it's 'See you soon.'" So much of my growth has come directly from him, and this one will stick with me as well.

This week I had some amazing conversations with some outstanding people. On Monday I met with Richard, and he gave me some tremendous advice on how to leverage my skillset to set myself apart for future opportunities. I also had a chance to talk with Kim at Accenture to learn more about the organization and explore potential fits for my experience. I had an awesome chat with LTG(R) Mayville, my former Division Commander from when I was in Afghanistan. He was so kind with his time and seeing his path and work with the organizations he supports was inspiring. I also had the chance to meet with Bryan from Seton Hall, and he's also an Army Baseball Alumni! He's doing some amazing work in the leader-development space, and it was a blast to learn more about his journey. I cannot tell you enough how impressive the Buccino Leadership Institute is; more industry leaders need to know about the stellar people coming out of this program.

In between all of this, I "cleared post" and got ready for Friday's pack-out. I also had the chance to say goodbye to the rugby team at the annual end-of-season banquet. The team has come so far, and I cannot wait to see them continue to climb and get better every day. They have a rock-solid culture, and they are destined to be even better next season. They also gave me a very nice going away gift, and I'm so thankful for the honor to work with the program these last few years.

I happened to run into my old boss, Adisa King, which was completely random! It was good to catch up and hear about his next assignment in Hawaii. This was an awesome week full of a lot of different emotions, but time to get to work for the move!

WHAT I'M READING AND LEARNING:

I finished the *Power of Vulnerability* and started *Thinking Fast and Slow*. I've listened to a couple of podcasts from Dr. Kahneman (and we use some of his work for our course text), so it's been fun to read the source material.

SELF-REFLECTION(S) OF THE WEEK:

West Point has been an amazing assignment, and so much of what I've learned here I plan to carry forward to my professional career. Interestingly, the bulk of my growth I've found post-cadet time, given that I've had the opportunity to reflect and understand where I've come from. I want to figure out a way to continue to give back to the Academy, and I think I have some unique ideas I'll start working on in a few months.

DID I SUCCEED IN MY PREVIOUS GOAL(S):

I did and was even able to complete some extra stuff to prep for the pack out of our household goods three days earlier than expected!

GOALS FOR NEXT WEEK:

Pack the house, enjoy McKinley's dance recital, eat into a coma at MEAT FEST 2021, have an amazing fifth birthday for McKinley, and spend quality time with my mom and our friends before we leave. I'm not committing to anything other than moving next week so we can get on the road!

INSPIRATION, PASSION, OR EXCITEMENT OF THE WEEK:

Two things. First was my mom getting to see Maddie, whom she hadn't seen for over a year due to COVID-19. Also seeing McKinley give grandma the biggest hug ever was so amazing. The second was something that COL Marson said in his speech to the rugby team: "You are above no man, and no man is above you." That has been rattling around in my head since he said it, and I plan to keep that quote with me.

GRATITUDE:

Thanks to Richard for having a 20+ minute networking meeting with me and teaching me more about outplacement firms and the power of transition coaching. Thanks to Kim for taking the time to talk to me more about Accenture. Thanks to LTG(R) Mayville for being so gracious with his time and talking Big Red One shop with me. Thanks to Bryan for his work in developing leaders and our discussion. Thanks to the Army Men's Rugby Team, especially the graduating "firsties" and Coaches Sherman and Sumsion. Thanks to the Department of Behavioral Sciences and Leadership, especially Everett Spain, Brian Reed, Todd Woodruff, Russ Lemler, Travis Tilman, Jason Bogardus, Ed Hudelson, Jordan Terry, Kim Cowan, Brian Gaudette, and Jess Gathers for their incredible support over the last year. So many others have helped me along the way in the department, and I am so thankful for the honor to have worked among some true giants.

IMPOSTER SYNDROME FIGHT:

You'll never see talk to these people again, they're going to forget you as soon as you walk out the door.

REFLECTION EXERCISE: COMBINING THE BIG WHEEL AND VENN DIAGRAM OF CAREER SATISFACTION

Let's start to put more pieces together and reflect. After you figure out the driving wheel, take a look back at your notes from the Venn Diagram of Career Satisfaction.

- Where are you aligned?

- Misaligned?

- Where do you need more research?

- What were your biggest surprises?

- What have you learned about your next steps?

- What _are_ your next steps?

Get specific; things are starting to get real.

REFLECTION EXERCISE:
COMBINING THE BIG WHEEL AND VENN DIAGRAM

Areas of Alignment	Areas of Misalignment

Where do I need to research more?

What was the biggest surprise?

What have I learned?

What are my next steps?

Author's Note: At this stage of my transition, I started moving from West Point, NY to Friso, TX. Because we were traveling as a family and the (spoiler alert) trauma of moving during the pandemic, the posts were much shorter for a month.

Post 22:
REAR VIEW MIRROR

Date: May 28, 2021

Different entry this week because I'm on the road and am operating off an iPad for the next couple of weeks.

Lots of ups (McKinley dance recital, farewell BBQ, seeing the rugby team commissioning ceremony) with some downs (saying goodbye to friends, an absolutely miserable pack-out experience). Even with that, I said my last words to West Point at Trophy Point. Because the move was so slow and horrible, I didn't get to have a more memorable last day, but I drove out of the gate for the last time as an Army Officer. It was surreal and still hasn't sunk in. As a cadet, we all talked about how exhilarating it would be to see West Point in our rear-view mirror, but this has been our home for over eight years and doing it the second time was incredibly sad. This is where Drew and I have spent the majority of our relationship together and our professional time in the military. We met here, raised kids here, and owe so much to the Academy. We will be back, but for now it's time to focus on the road ahead.

We're spending a couple of days at Gettysburg to decompress and then making the slow journey across the country. I might post some additional photos as we go or do one big post when we finish the drive. Here's to the start of Adventure 2.0!

IMPOSTER SYNDROME FIGHT:
You're forgetting something, you always do.

REFLECTION QUESTION:

What organizations do you plan to join when you get settled in?

Post 23:
1,502 MILES

Date: June 4, 2021

After seven days, 1,502 miles, with a lot of time in hotel rooms and pools, we made it to Drew's parents in Oklahoma to officially start terminal leave. As of writing this post, I'm signed out. It has been a wild ride, and it still feels surreal. I haven't fully processed it yet and likely won't for a while.

The photo is of me and Maddie at the OKC Science Museum recreating a photo that McKinley and I took before we went to West Point. Full circle!

Time to grow out my hair and fill in a beard. I'm off to the pool! See you all next week when I move into the new house in Texas!

IMPOSTER SYNDROME FIGHT:
There are too many unknowns out there, you can't possible figure this out.

REFLECTION EXERCISE: STRATEGIC NETWORKING

Originally, I thought to add this to the beginning of the book. Why? Because frankly, it is the single most important thing you can do during a career transition. Building a network is invaluable. It connects you with other people across industries, businesses, and backgrounds. It shows you what's out there, gives you contacts, and can help you open previously locked doors.

But how do we optimize this in an effective and efficient way?

In the Needs Survey exercise, I mentioned doing research into the roles that you are interested in to identify businesses and people to locate position information and credentials to acquire. I also briefly discussed how important it is to connect with those people to learn more details about the inner workings of the job and the business. This is the next step.

No matter the stage in your career shift or transition adventure, networking is critical. *How* to network is a different beast. The ultimate goal is simple: bypass the algorithm to get your résumé in the hands of a human, preferably the one making the hiring decision.

For those unfamiliar, there are three key things to understand about job listings and the hiring process.

1. Algorithms aren't your friends. For most large organizations, especially ones where you upload a résumé onto a website (then subsequently have to redo your gosh darned résumé anyway!), the initial screen is done by an algorithm. Most job descriptions are copied and pasted,

and often don't match the actual requirements of the position. But that doesn't matter to a computer program. It scrapes your résumé looking for key terms that match the job description and will immediately screen you out for an arbitrary or unexplainable reason. You can't control this, and often the people hiring are unaware and can't control it either.

2. **People are your friends.** Strategic networking is where you make your money. In my adventures, I read the *20-Minute Networking Meeting (20MNM)* and was fortunate enough to speak with the authors. Your interactions, optimized with the tips from *20MNM*, will allow you to better engage with networking contacts. Even if they aren't part of the hiring process, if you impress them, and you have a job in mind on their "job board," they may be willing to walk your résumé directly to the hiring manager. Shoot, many big companies have an incentive program for referral bonuses, so it actually helps them out! Having a person inside the company take your résumé directly to the decision maker increases your success rate for hiring as well as bolsters your network further. Win, win, win! Here's another layer. Some organizations have unlisted positions or anticipated vacancies that will never show up on a job website. If the people you speak with identify your strengths and see you as a potential fit for an unlisted position, now you're not competing with anyone. Some

call this the "black book" of jobs, but really, it's just a way to avoid competition for you!

3. You are your best friend. This sounds weird, and candidly it doesn't work for everyone. Sometimes, you can craft your own job. If you come from a unique background and have particular skills, your ability to explain that may actually trigger the organization to build a role to fit *you*. "That can't be true," I hear you saying. Oh yeah? That's what I did. The company that hired me had never hired a veteran before. At the point of writing this book, I'm the only non-PhD consultant in the organization. I shared with them my background in teaching, training, and organizational psychology. During my interview process, on top of the typical suite of assessments and screening, I was required to teach the entire company a class of my choosing. They saw my background and skillset as an opportunity to expand their business into an area they weren't capturing as well as they could. So, they brought me on to build out a better training program and to lead workshops to help other leaders get better. I may hold the title of "Consultant," but the role I fill was custom-built for me and continues to evolve as I leverage more of my talents and experience to improve the business. It can be done, I promise.

With those rules out of the way, here are my tips:

- If you know what you're looking for, find people that fit those positions and connect with them on LinkedIn. Don't just send a connection request, write a note asking politely to have the opportunity to talk with them to learn more. Being interested in them and their work is an easy way to get them to respond, and you get to learn more about what that person's day-to-day looks like!

- If you can't get traction using the above method and you know you're interested in a particular company, you can leverage the search function on LinkedIn. Find the company, go to the people tab, then use the filters to identify commonalities to your background. Are you a veteran? Look for folks that have "veterans" in their title in that company. Member of a specific organization? Dig around and find someone who is as well. Establishing that common ground can increase your chances of a return contact.

- For my transitioning service members, look for veteran hiring managers or other related titles. Many large organizations put veteran hiring under Diversity, Equity, and Inclusion, so check corporate websites to see what info you can dig out. Many large companies will list the contacts for vets to reach out to, and many even have veteran hiring and/or training programs!

- If all else fails, track down people in Human Resources in the organization, preferably hiring managers. Again, engaging them to talk about the company to see if it's a good fit is a great lead-in to have a conversation. If they agree to a call, leverage the techniques from *20MNM* to make this more impactful!

Okay, that was a lot, how do we turn this into action? Simple. Make yourself a goal to reach out to three to five people on LinkedIn *per day*. Oof, I just felt a disturbance in the force as introverts tensed up and got anxious just thinking about talking to another human they don't know. Yup, I said simple, but I didn't say easy. Frankly, this is a numbers game. The percentage of people who will respond depends on your ability to strategically network. The percentage of people who have conversations with you may be small. But each one is another step towards the ultimate goal of your next career. Take a small step every day and before you know it, you'll have walked a mile. Get after it!

REFLECTION EXERCISE:
STRATEGIC NETWORKING

What is my daily contact goal?
I will contact _____ people per day

Organization of Interest	Contact to Engage

Post 24:
NEW HOUSE, NEW LIFE

Date: June 11, 2021

Short post today as I take a quick break from cleaning up the house to prep for the rest of the family and furniture to arrive early next week.

Finally made it to Frisco and signed for our new house. It's been a wild ride traveling, and now the hard work starts. I'm doing easy stuff (signing up for Costco membership) and difficult things like getting childcare figured out.

The new house is a huge step up for us in a very quiet neighborhood with so many neat places nearby. I can't wait to take the kids around to see the sights and explore the cool restaurants.

The next step is to get our furniture in and get the office back up and running so I can continue to search for my next career. My goal for the week is to finish Chris Coultas, Ph.D., and Leadership Worth Following, LLC's book *Driven, Not Drained* while I enjoy my new patio.

IMPOSTER SYNDROME FIGHT:

How are you going to make ends meet, you don't have a clue what you're doing.

REFLECTION QUESTION:
Who has been most supportive during this process, and why?

Post 25:
MOVING NIGHTMARE

Date: June 18, 2021

Short post this week because, despite my household goods being expected to be delivered on the 10th, the company moved it to the 15th, then failed to deliver them. Now we're stuck in limbo until the 22nd when our stuff (supposedly) arrives. We're making the best of a bad situation by exploring the local area, but we really want to put our house back together.

I have some exciting events scheduled for next week, but arguably the most exciting is getting the kids back in daycare! We were so fortunate to find a place that is just around the corner and can take both of them.

See you all next week, and back to managing the chaos!

IMPOSTER SYNDROME FIGHT:
What makes you think you're good enough?

REFLECTION QUESTION:

How are you going to thank everyone for helping you in this journey?

_____
_____
_____
_____
_____
_____
_____
_____
_____
_____

Post 26:
COMING TOGETHER NICELY

Date: June 25, 2021

WHAT I DID THIS WEEK:

Back to the regularly scheduled structure! What a week. With our household goods delivered on Tuesday, we've been slowly putting the house back together. I'm down to just a few rooms left, but I hope to finish the bulk today so I can enjoy the weekend.

In between throwing around boxes and arranging drawers, I had the chance to sit down and have coffee with Dan. His deep connections in Frisco and openness to bringing me and my wife into the fold were so amazing. I'm extremely excited to see more of the area, and he shared so many amazing opportunities to help benefit the local area through volunteering and other cool opportunities. I also had the chance to talk to Pete, who opened himself to be part of my support network for my transition. My buddy Brian pointed Pete my way, and I had an awesome time getting to know him and hope we can help each other down the road!

I was fortunate enough to get to meet and ask questions of some of the amazing people who work at Leadership Worth Following. Learning more about them, their organization, and their passions was a blast. They are a top-tier group of people with an outstanding mission. I was able to pitch a class on how character is taught at West Point, and in true fashion, my slides decided to die on me. Oh well! I learned a ton about how they view character and leadership development, which was super enjoyable.

WHAT I'M READING AND LEARNING:

I'm nearly done with *Driven, Not Drained*, which is an excellent book. Even if you don't take the DRiV assessment prior to reading, you can still learn a tremendous amount about yourself and members of your team with anecdotes, testimonies, and tips. I also have been going through *Thinking Fast and Slow* while I unpack stuff, which has been nice to revisit.

SELF-REFLECTION(S) OF THE WEEK:

Time to cut the excuses, quit drinking, and eat healthily. Period. I must be better.

DID I SUCCEED IN MY PREVIOUS GOAL(S):

I didn't really have any, but I've gotten quite a few rooms fully complete and organized, so I'm happy with my personal progress!

GOALS FOR NEXT WEEK:

Zero alcohol. 1,500 net calories per day. Finish the move. Reconnect and set up discussions with the list of ~20 people I have on my notes sheet (discussions not required by next week).

INSPIRATION, PASSION, OR EXCITEMENT OF THE WEEK:

Both kids love their new daycare! We were very nervous, but of course, kids are super resilient and will always inspire you. A bonus to the place we selected is that they send us photos throughout the day of Maddie, so we get little snap shots into what she's up to!

GRATITUDE:

Thanks to Dan McCall for your time and opening your heart to us. I look forward to staying tied in with you to support the veteran community here in Frisco. Thanks to Peter Kohler for his willingness to help me during the transition. Thanks to the team at Leadership Worth Following. In particular, Dale Thompson, thank you for taking additional time to chat with me and give me feedback!

Now, back to organizing!

IMPOSTER SYNDROME FIGHT:
They're going to see right through you.

REFLECTION EXERCISE: WHO ARE YOU? PART DEUX

You've had time to reflect, practice, and learn. Ideally, you have a clearer picture of yourself. I had you start off with your professional and personal high points, as well as a metaphor. Revisit those high points—is there anything you would change now that you've thought through things? Let's take a look back at where you started with your original three-sentence definition of who you are. As you read through your writing,

- What resonates most strongly?

- Least strongly?

- What do you need to add?

- Remove?

- Change?

Let's add another metaphor into the mix. Metaphorically, how would you describe your journey to this point? I shared mine in the intro of this book: I banged my head against the wall over and over again until it fell over, my hope is to show you the door just to the right. What's yours?

Let's refine with the same prompt: In three sentences or less, who are you?

REFLECTION EXERCISE:
WHO ARE YOU? - PART 2

Who are you? - Initial attempt

What resonates strongest?

What needs to change?

How would you metaphorically describe your journey to this point?

Who are you? - Attempt 2

Post 27:
ACCEPTING AN OFFER!

Date: July 2, 2021

WHAT I DID THIS WEEK:

This was a great week to catch up with some amazing folks. On Monday I had a fun chat with Charles, who is a fellow veteran and a TC alum. He is doing some incredible work with Accenture, and it was awesome to get to learn more about him. After an invite from Dan, I attended the Frisco VFW monthly meeting and met some wonderful people, including David, a fellow grad who is crushing it in the DFW area.

I also had the chance to talk with Rob on FaceTime, Doug over text, Gina via email, Scott on the Phone, and Bill on Zoom. I spoke to all of these amazing people to get their advice, because… I've accepted an offer to work with Leadership Worth Following as a consultant! I began this whole endeavor on December 30th and starting at the end of this month I'll be working with LWF. I am so incredibly thrilled to join the team and hit the ground running. I cannot wait.

WHAT I'M READING AND LEARNING:

I took a break from the more technical reading and jumped into *Hail Mary* by Andy Weir. Great book so far, and I highly recommend it!

SELF-REFLECTION(S) OF THE WEEK:

The work I put in to clarify my purpose through the COMMIT foundation and reading *Leading from Purpose* was invaluable. I knew what kind of organization I wanted to work for, and I went for it. Also, leveraging the skills that Scott taught me through the AOG career services program was invaluable. I'm learning to network via *20MNM* and practicing over and over again boosted my confidence. I plan on going into more detail about overall "If I could go back in time" in another post next week.

DID I SUCCEED IN MY PREVIOUS GOAL(S):

Nope! I was able to reconnect with quite a few people, but I weakly decided to celebrate with some nice beer after receiving the offer. I'm going to take the holiday weekend to celebrate, then it's back to zero alcohol and 1,500 net calories again!

GOALS FOR NEXT WEEK:

Enjoy the holiday with the kids and then hit the books hard to catch up on my Agile Certified Practitioners class. I also want to analyze the key things that I feel helped me achieve my goal of working for a company I believe in.

INSPIRATION, PASSION, OR EXCITEMENT OF THE WEEK:
I got a job. I'm flippin' excited!

GRATITUDE:
Thanks so much to Charles for his time. Thanks to Dan for introducing me to so many amazing people at the VFW. Thanks to David for his willingness to help ease my transition into the area (and dedicating himself to being a golfing buddy!). Thanks to those who helped me confirm my decision to work with LWF: Rob for his amazing support through the transition process, Doug for giving me some amazing advice and wisdom, Gina for always bringing positivity and believing in me, and Scott for his sage advice, and Bill for his incredible support and passion for helping me out. Having a group like you all in my corner cheering me on helped me feel safe and supported during this difficult time. Finally, thanks to the team at LWF! I am going to bring the energy to them, and I truly cannot thank Myranda and Dale for bringing me onto their already-amazing team!

IMPOSTER SYNDROME FIGHT:
You're going to let everyone down, just like the last time.

REFLECTION QUESTION:

You're at the end of this journey (for now), what does success look like for you? How does it compare to when you started?

REFLECTION EXERCISE: ELEVATOR PITCH V1.0

We're towards the end of this journey together, so let's dust off the elevator pitch one last time. Well, I say one last time, but to be fair that's not exactly true. There's a reason why I didn't title this "The Final Elevator Pitch" or "Elevator Pitch, Final, Final, FINAL". Your elevator pitch evolved throughout the first two iterations, I assume, and it will continue to do so. You will likely need to tailor it to the conversation, the person, and the organization. You might pick up a new certification or have something bubble to the surface that you want to add. That's great!

To this point, you've learned a lot about yourself and what you want. Let's put another layer of polish on your pitch. Start with re-reading your Version 0.9, then answer the same questions we did going from V0.1 to V0.9.

- What sticks out as an absolute keeper?

- What needs to get removed?

- Do you need to add anything new that you identified recently?

- How can you clarify it for your audience?

Now, go stand in front of a mirror and read it. Seriously. It helps, I promise.

- How does it sound? Is it you? Like, your authentic self?

- What language can you change to make it flow better? This pitch may open the door to your next career, so how can you give it that extra punch that might land with the listener?

- What are you going to change?

Excellent. Now go read it to someone else. Ask for their honest feedback. Don't settle for "Oh, it's great!" Ask for specific feedback about what worked well and what didn't. Keep in mind that it will not land perfectly for everyone, but the feedback is still valid. Listen, understand, ask questions, and refine. Get better. Every time, get better.

Put your pitch into a document and save it as "Elevator Pitch V1.0". If you're a digital hoarder like me, save a copy of your previous version and rename a new document after each minor update after this by changing the decimal point (1.1, 1.2…). Major revisions, change the number (2.0, 3.0…). It's fun to look back on the progress you've made, I promise.

Now it's time to get out there and test it out. When you schedule time with people, after initial pleasantries, lead with your pitch. Get some reps in. Bonus challenge: ask for feedback on the pitch. Don't ever be afraid to ask how you can improve. The person you're talking with already gave you time to help you in some capacity, I'm certain they'll be willing to help you some more. And, spoiler alert, it shows you care and want to be better.

I don't know of many organizations that don't value a prospective hire who shows a "growth mindset" and is "open to feedback" in just an intro discussion.

REFLECTION EXERCISE:
ELEVATOR PITCH V1.0

Positive opener and gratitude

Highlights
(use short reminder phrases)
1.
2.
3.
4.

Skills
1.
2.
3.
4.
5.
6.

Personal Story

The "Ask"

Gratitude!

Post 28:
IF I COULD START OVER

Date: July 9, 2021

This will be a different post this week as I want to review how I went from the start of my transition to the beginning of Adventure 2.0. Initially, I had the idea to build a link chart that showed how all my conversations led to finding a job. I had in my mind a giant spider web with one line going through the middle. However, that's not how it worked out. Interestingly, where I am now coming back to leveraging techniques that Scott taught me during the very first conversation we had together. I don't want to give away the entire story up front, because while his advice was directly responsible for helping me find my new role, there's so much I would have changed.

Before we begin, for those who are unfamiliar with my background I'll give you the "elevator pitch." This is a version I used for the majority of my conversations with people, and how I developed it is something that I'll cover shortly:

IF I COULD START OVER

I have been in the army for more than 15 years, most of which as an officer, specializing in leading organizations from 19 to more than 1,100 people in extremely demanding and often dangerous circumstances. After competing for and being accepted to return to West Point as a TAC officer, I earned my master's in organizational psychology from Columbia. At West Point, using my graduate degree and leadership experience, I focused on leveraging mentorship and executive coaching skills to develop future army officers, and I eventually was selected to serve as a military leadership instructor in the department of behavioral sciences and leadership. Despite a promising career ahead of me, I decided to leave the military to support my wife's career aspirations so that my young daughters can see their mom work.

So now that we all are on the same page as to who I am and why I left the Army, here's what I would do, when, and why. Oh, and for some common terminology. When I say transition date, that's the day you want to start your new life. Hard to pin down that for each person, for some, that's after their official terminal-leave completion, for some, that's when they start terminal leave, and for me, it ended up being about midway through terminal leave after I took a couple of months off.

1. Find your purpose

    a) **What:** Read Leading from Purpose by Nick Craig (Thanks Nick!)

    b) **When:** Immediately (good for anyone to do right now, but this should be your first step). I'd suggest at least one year from your transition date.

    c) **Why:** You won't know what you want if you don't know who you are. Defining your purpose (mine as of now is to help people level up from home cooks to professional chefs using the ingredients in their own kitchens) will give you clarity on the things you want to do.

2. Get an accountability partner

    a) **What:** Get an executive coach to help you define your core values. (Thanks, Hamaria, COMMIT, and Kyle!)

    b) **When:** About one year from the transition date, although if you're able to do this now (even if you're not transitioning to a new career), it's invaluable.

    c) **Why:** Again, knowing who you are is critical. If you are clear on your values, as you research organizations, you'll see alignment and can hunt for a good culture fit.

    d) **Resources available:** USMA grads have AOG Career Services, which has a deal with Korn Ferry

Advance for free coaching. I also recommend the COMMIT Foundation, as they help you establish your values and purpose in life via the Pursue Your Purpose (PYP) modules. I know there are other things out there for veterans, but those two were so great for me.

3. Be a better networker

   a) **What:** Read *The 20-Minute Networking Meeting* (thanks to Marcia and Nathan!)

   b) **When:** Ideally before you start networking. I didn't start this until about midway through my journey, and I was not as efficient as I could have been with my conversations.

   c) **Why:** The tips that the authors use genuinely work. I created a framework (template) word document that I used prior to each conversation, which I tailored to fit each person I talked with based on my research into their organization and personal background. Being deliberate about this worked for two reasons: 1) I respected people's time more effectively, and 2) I asked better questions allowing for deeper discussions.

   d) What this looked like in action:

      i) Gratitude and personal connection (found through LinkedIn)

ii) Elevator pitch (a version of the one I used above, tweaked based on who I was talking to, such as more or less military jargon if a veteran or not)

iii) Question 1

iv) Question 2

v) Question 3

vi) Question 4: The "ask" (typically asking for another connection in a role/organization closer to what I was looking for)

vii) Question 5: How can I help you?

viii) Close/follow up/gratitude

4. Get some career mentorship (this one is a bit specific to USMA graduates, but hopefully the skills are beneficial to more)

a) **What:** Contact AOG Career Services (thanks, Scott!)

b) **When:** About a year out from the transition date, with more focus starting at about the six-month mark

c) **Why:** They will get you set up with Korn Ferry Advance coaching, get you set up on how to translate your résumé, and help you spruce up your LinkedIn profile. They'll also give you some good tips on apps to use, such as Handshake, and get you dialed into the Service Academy Career Conferences.

d) **Similar resource:** Hire Heroes USA is another resource that I leveraged that was super helpful that covers a lot of the same bases.

5. Chip away at your résumé

   a) **What:** Prep your résumé

   b) **When:** About six months from the transition date, but earlier will be better if you're diving into networking

   c) **Why:** I had the most anxiety about this, in particular with a military background. I found it really difficult to translate my experience into corporate speak without sounding fake or like I was coming up with a bunch of BS. If you feel the same way, you'll probably have about 20 revisions, with a different version for each job you apply for.

6. Get a certification tied to your goals

   a) **What:** Sign up for (https://ivmf.syracuse.edu/) and the Onward 2 Opportunity to get certified in something. I went with PMI-ACP, and I wish I would have started sooner.

b) **When:** Start around the one-year mark so you can get your cohort. I ended up doing this too late, and I had to delay my completion due to the hellish moving situation.

c) **Why:** It's free, and you get trained and certified in something that will set you apart!

7. Do the work

    a) **What:** Set goals to network with a couple of people a week, do the work to figure out who you are and what you want, and take copious notes. I'll give my stats at the end of this post.

    b) **When:** Ongoing, until you find your next career!

    c) **Why:** If you're like me, learning more about people is fascinating. You start to understand and pick up more from their industries, make connections, and build a natural network.

8. Hiring Our Heroes/Career Skills Program

    a) **What:** An incredible organization coupled with CSP to allow you a good chunk of time to do an "unpaid internship" ideally in a job you will be offered following your internship.

    b) **When:** Research about a year out, ensuring you line up all the paperwork (needs some high-level signatures) and that you're finding great options for your career aspirations. HoH helps remove some of the personal legwork via an interview and matching process, but there's no shortage of opportunities out there if you go looking.

c) Why: An extra four to six months of military pay while you get experience in corporate America. I rolled the dice based on timing (and a lot of the organizations I was looking into didn't allow for unpaid internships), but I would definitely push harder into this world if I didn't feel as confident.

9. Other Random Tips

a) Find companies you're interested in on LinkedIn, then search for people who are veterans, went to college with you, or are "veteran hiring managers." Those folks are tremendous advocates for you and can help you connect with hiring managers or people filling positions while helping translate your experience. Lots of larger organizations have veteran's groups under Diversity and Inclusion with info on their website.

b) Set up searches on LinkedIn to notify you when jobs are available that meet specific requirements. Sometimes the most random phrases that you save can bring up great results (or vice versa). For example, with my grad degree in org psych I found the search term "Succession

Planning" to be very effective. Conversely, "Leadership Development" was very unhelpful, as it pulled in a lot of leadership training programs for interns. Be deliberate about your search terms!

c) Have thick skin. While I always knew this would be difficult, I always had it in my mind that when the time came for me to leave the military, the USMA AOG would have some grads show up in my email inbox with a six-figure job. I would argue that in my timing I'm one of the most difficult to find a job (not a young JMO but not a retired former battalion or higher commander), but I had no clue it would be as hard as it was. Be prepared to have your ego smashed over and over again. Of the people I reached out to, I'd say about 20% responded, and only about half of those set up meetings with me. I am forever grateful for those who took the time to chat with me, without them I wouldn't be where I'm at now.

d) View every engagement as a chance to get better, and don't be afraid to ask for feedback. I had a few discussions I felt I did very well at, and even more I struggled through. I'd take the chance to see where I could refine my story, increase the impact, and try again the next time.

Okay, so now onto the fun stuff. How did I land my offer? At the recommendation of Scott, I Googled management consulting firms in the DFW area, picked through them, and found one whose mission and vision spoke to me. I had googled companies before, but by this point I knew I wanted to work for an organization who believed that character matters, that is focused on teamwork, and that has high performers pushing toward a bold vision. When I found Leadership Worth Following (LWF), I used the techniques to search through their employees that Scott taught me, and I sent out a few messages hoping to connect and ask more questions. Fortunately for me, Trish responded, and she met with me! We had a great chat (and continue to have frequent catch-up sessions), and she served as a champion for me through the whole process. With her assistance, she helped me connect with some other amazing people to learn more about other potential opportunities, and with the CEO and President of LWF. After multiple discussions and other hiring-related interview things, I received an offer!

While it's easy to make it seem like fate, I will say that when I talked with Trish, by that point I had been working daily for more than four months on preparing for the transition. I had multiple iterations of practice discussions, coaching, learning about myself, and networking calls. I felt very confident because of what I had been taught and the work I put in. I had page after page of stories tied to accomplishments throughout my career, thought through my strengths and weaknesses, and had amazing people provide me advice over a nine-month span. I cannot thank everyone enough for their support during this process.

THE FINAL STATS:

First Discussion: October 13th, 2020, at a coffee shop in Cornwall, NY with Dr. Tony Burgess. He connected me with Rob Campbell, who served as a mentor and advocate this whole time.

Total discussions related to transition: More than 88 (that's how many Word documents I have saved with notes). Important to understand, after I read the 20MNM my skills and confidence in networking jumped considerably.

Résumé revisions: 17 (including one by Hire Heroes USA and a one-on-one with Scott Vedder)

Résumés adapted for specific job applications: 15

LinkedIn Connections made: More than 200 (rough estimate, likely closer to 300+), many I still stay in touch with consistently. I've made some great friends and mentors on this journey with whom I will continue to cultivate deep and long-lasting relationships.

LinkedIn Posts/Articles: 28 written, which started as a way to hold myself accountable but ended up helping others also navigate this crazy journey. Unintentionally this became my brand, and I hope reduced some of the anxiety associated with big life changes. If I can do it, so can you!

This will serve as the final entry in this series. Next week I head to Alaska to help my mom with some work at High Lake, then I come home to get a haircut (and make a final decision on the beard) and start work! I am ready to hit the ground sprinting and bringing energy to my new teammates. Thanks to everyone who followed along and rooted for me, and thanks specifically to everyone who assisted me on my journey to find Adventure 2.0

IMPOSTER SYNDROME FIGHT:
This is done. I'm over the imposter syndrome. It's time to be confident in myself because I know who I am. I know what I can do. I know my strengths and my weaknesses. That's okay. I have a lot to offer. I am ready to push past this and slay the beast. Confidence. Humility. Pride. Grace. Growth.

REFLECTION QUESTION:

What are the three most valuable things from this experience? (Experience can be defined as using the tools in this book, your own transition, or your own reflective journey)

REFLECTION EXERCISE: THE FEAR GAP AND THE LEAP OF COURAGE

I love intent-based leadership where people give me an end state and give me the freedom to find my own way (within boundaries, of course). To this point, we've explored quite a bit of your journey to get to where you are and reflect on where you want to be. Let's take that a step further using this guide.

I want you to visualize your end state. Close your eyes and think about when you'd feel satisfied. For me, that was owning a home, moving in, my wife having a meaningful career, and my kids being in school.

Now look back on your Needs Survey to pull in your KSAOs. Your experience. Even your anxiety and worry about the uncertainty that you're experiencing. My fears during this process are expressed through the imposter syndrome fights, I suspect you might feel some of the same emotions.

- What do I bring to the table?

- What can I draw from my experience to help me be successful?

- What are my fears?

Imagine now that you're standing on a platform, with your end state perched atop a higher platform. Between your current state and your end state is the "Fear Gap." That's the pit filled with your worries, anxiety, worst-case scenarios, and past failures.

There's no way to get to the other side, and you're terrified of what's below.

To hell with that. Think back to your experience and grab onto something difficult that you overcame. You have done something difficult that seemed impossible at the time, I guarantee it. How did it happen? It wasn't one huge jump to success. There was a step-by-step process to get you there.

That step-by-step process has already started, assuming of course you aren't slacking on your reflection and these exercises. Each of these steps is the next stair you're building in front of you. Each conversation where you learn is another stair. Each revision of your résumé. Every mistake is an opportunity to reflect on how to get better.

But no matter how much you prepare, there's a jump that must happen. You must take the "Leap of Courage" over the "Fear Gap."

That time may not be now, but it's coming. Keep growing yourself and getting your family ready. But the time will come to make the leap, and you need to remember the phrase: "Just do the damn thing."

REFLECTION EXERCISE:
THE FEAR GAP AND THE LEAP OF COURAGE

Visualized Endstate	
What do I bring to the table?	What can I draw from?
What are my fears?	

You can build up confidence all you want, but at certain point you must take a leap.

Find the courage and *"Do the Damn Thing!"*

CONCLUSION

At this point, you've reflected on 15 different questions and completed 13 exercises. Time to get meta and reflect on the reflections.

Look back at how you defined success at the beginning and end of this process. What are the biggest differences between what you thought at the start and finish of this journey? What stayed the same? This clarity should bring you comfort, you've learned more about yourself.

Look at your elevator pitch V0.1 and V1.0. What is most drastically different? You've put that clarity about yourself and what you want into words that are ready to share.

Look back at your Needs Survey and your combination of the Big Wheel and Venn Diagram. These are the actual things you bring to the table, and the tangible direction of what's getting you there. Ideally, that Big Wheel takes you to the nexus of the Venn Diagram. You now have better knowledge of your next steps and scoping in your work moving forward.

Look at the starting and ending "Who are you?". What speaks deepest to you in your core? What gives you great pride? Why? This is your guiding light. This is what you can always fall back on when the other things may fall a bit short of your expectations. You don't always have to link this to your work, because your life's purpose is about more than a job.

Last, take a look at the Fear Gap and the Leap of Courage. What fears remain? What anxiety exists? What's still uncomfortable? There will always be a gap, it can't be closed entirely. But you've built additional steps to get to your end state and your future self. You're standing with your toes on the edge, and all it takes is a leap.

For some things you're trying to achieve, you might fall short. That's not failure, it's a learning opportunity. Don't succumb to the fear, do the work. Grow, get better, and get back with your toes on the edge.

This book is named *Brute Force and Ignorance* because it's often the way I tackle tasks. I may not know what I'm doing, but I'll do it over and over again until I succeed. I've shared my stories and exercises in the hopes that you can find an easier path than the one I picked. You will have success and failures, but you are unique, and your journey is your own.

Regardless, don't forget, above all else: "Just do the damn thing."

Zach

GRATITUDE AND ACKNOWLEDGEMENTS

I don't pretend to be an expert in this topic, I'm just a person who wanted to share and help. I'm blessed to have amazing people who supported me during a very difficult time in my life. I still rely on many of them to this day. This process gave me life-long friends and mentors.

I deliberately left in their names in this book to express my gratitude again. But I'd like to highlight some folks again (or for the first time) that helped me during the development of this book.

First, thanks to Al Chase for his aggressive suggestion to start the project, Rob Campbell for his inspiration and resources, and Scott Leishman for his wisdom and support.

Thanks to the people who took the time to read through the draft to provide me feedback, Chad Plenge, Trish Perryman, Natasha Orslene, and Tom Murphy.

Thank you to the people who served as my pilot testers for the exercises to help me dial them in to increase their clarity and impact.

Thank you to Christine Nicholson for helping me stare my imposter syndrome in the face, and for the inspiration to add my fight with it to the book.

Thanks to those to provided me with insights and advice throughout this journey:

Drew Mierva, Matt Rosebaugh, Scott Leishman, COL Everett Spain, Gina Buontempo, Rob Campbell, Beth Wetzler, Daniel Liss, Mark Raschke, Josh Kopsie, Hamaria Crockett, Brooke Jones-Chinetti, Nick Loudon, Freddie Kim, Adam Dikker, Tim Dunn, Reggie Mills, Bethany Biszko, Scott Vedder, Donnie LaGrange, Rob Stanton, Kyle Moses, Rick Garcia, Brennan Randal, Ross Skilling, Brandon Walker, Yvette Benevidez Garcia, Donnie Seidle, Shawn Robertson, Kate Migliaro, John Roper, Neil Lynn, Carrie Jablonski, Tom Giboney, Russ Medina, Chris White and Jerrod Gaertner, Rod Hairston, Russ Lemler, Nick Cahill, Jonna Eckenrod, Rob Hill, Mitali Bose, Bob Carl, Tod Willoughby, Al Chase, Josh Bowen, Lindsey Bowen, Natasha Orslene, Jim Hughes, Mark Fogel, Kelly Swaintek, Len East, Brandon Brown, Nick Craig, Dr. Marcia Ballinger and Nathan Perez, Dave Bakkeby, Sydney Morris, Chad Plenge, Pat Coan, Indra Nooyi, Dr. Rebecca Stilwell, Aimee Lace, Jacquie Jordan, GEN Daryl Williams, Dr. Bill Pasmore, Trish Perryman, Don Byerly, Charles Browne, Mark McKearn, Ellen White, Danny Ballard, Sheri Winesett, Jackie Coan, Ken Killingsworth, Ben Dalton, Kayla D., Harris Fanaroff, Tyler Freeman, Will Dickson, Dale Thompson, Myranda Grayhek, Dave Oliver, Brian Boyson, Matt Sherman, Kyle Sumsion, Michel Smith, Steena Chandler, Julian Chender, Lauren Gold Miller, Jonathan Atwood, Jan

GRATITUDE AND ACKNOWLEDGEMENTS

Rutherford, Matt and Janet Biddick, Richard Dodson, Kim Beal, LTG(R) Bill Mayville, Bryan Price, Brian Reed, Todd Wodruff, Travis Tilman, Jason Bogardus, Ed Hudelson, Jordan Terry, Kim Cowan, Brian Gaudette, Jess Gathers, Dan McCall, Peter Kohler, Charles Newnam, and David Seals.

Shout out to anyone I didn't recognize who supported, championed, or followed along during the journey. My apologies if I missed anyone, chalk it up to getting hit in the head too many times!

Thank you to the team at Leadership Worth Following who provided me with support to build out these concepts, gave me a career to pursue my purpose, and allowed me to take this idea and use it to change leadership and change the world. Note: I parted ways with LWF to pursue my purpose on a much larger scale, but I still carry their spirit with me. I'm so grateful for the incredible people at LWF!

Special thanks to Everett Spain, whose teachings, mentorship, and love gave me so, so much.

Lastly, thank you to my family: my wife, Drew, for always being there to support me and being a tremendous role model for our girls; my daughters McKinley and Maddison for their amazing spirits; my brothers Luke and Jake, for all of the fun times; my mom, Michelle, for her undying love and the sacrifices she made for our family; and finally, Rob. No single person has shaped the leader and person I am today more than him. If you had to connect a line to who I am and where I came from, it all started with him.

I love you all.

Appendix 1:
EXECUTIVE CHECKLIST

When you're too busy to read the whole thing and want "the down-and-dirty."

SUGGESTED READING LIST

Designing Your Life by Bill Burnett
Leading from Purpose by Nick Craig
Atomic Habits by James Clear
Signs of a Great Résumé by Scott Vedder

TIPS

- Get an executive coach
- Define your purpose in life
- Network, network, network…strategically
- Conduct a survey of where you are and what you want, and identify the gap between

- Determine the important things you want out of your next job
- Create a time-based plan with all the tasks you need to complete
- Figure out what career satisfaction looks like for you
- Decide what's most important: where you want to go, what you want to do, or how much money you want to make
- Craft your résumé
- Create your elevator pitch
- Do the work
- Take the leap

Appendix 2:
CONSOLIDATED LIST OF RESOURCES

Here is a list of the critical books, agencies, or programs that supported me during my transition. I've also included some extras that I may not have used personally but that provide value to transitioning service members. All descriptions come from the resource's website.

The 20-Minute Networking Meeting
by Nathan A. Perez and Marcia Ballinger
"LEARN HOW TO...Be Concise": Have you ever led a meeting that went on too long? Learn to set an agenda and conduct a highly informative conversation [within] 20 minutes. Ask The Right Questions: The best conversations start with the best questions. The *20-Minute Networking Meeting* shows you how to construct such questions to lead a discussion. Avoid Common Mistakes: Small things like eye contact and expressing gratitude

leave a lasting impression about your character. Learn how to avoid common but costly mistakes."

American Corporate Partners
(https://www.acp-usa.org/)
"Founded in 2008, ACP aims to ease the transition from the military to the civilian workforce. ACP is the only nonprofit organization engaged in national corporate career counseling for our returning veterans and active-duty military spouses. More than 100 of America's finest companies support ACP. We are also proud to work with a variety of best-in-class veteran service organizations, professional groups, and military transition programs."

Atomic Habits
by James Clear
"*Atomic Habits* is the most comprehensive and practical guide on how to create good habits, break bad ones, and get one percent better every day. I do not believe you will find a more actionable book on the subject of habits and improvement. If you're having trouble changing your habits, the problem isn't you. The problem is your system."

Candorful
(https://www.candorful.org)
"We know firsthand the difficulties of military transition and the job search that follows. Job seekers who are Service Members or Veterans need to translate their experiences and skills to launch their career. Our mock interviews prepare them to make a great first impression

and get hired into the civilian workforce. The career transition road for non-military professionals isn't easy either. Practice interviews are the key to smoothing that career shift for those at risk."

COMMIT Foundation
(https://www.commitfoundation.org/)
"COMMIT seeks to provide high touch transition support that becomes the standard nationwide so veterans in all communities can access services helping them identify their passions, build strong networks, and leverage their skills in civilian careers."

D'Aniello Institute for Veterans & Military Families
(https://www.ivmf.syracuse.edu)
"The IVMF at Syracuse University is higher education's first interdisciplinary academic institute, singularly focused on advancing the post-service lives of the nation's military veterans and their families to serve those who have served."

Designing Your Life
by Bill Burnett and Dave Evans
"In this book, Bill Burnett and Dave Evans show us how design thinking can help us create a life that is both meaningful and fulfilling, regardless of who or where we are, what we do or have done for a living, or how young or old we are. The same design thinking responsible for amazing technology, products, and spaces can be used to design and build your career and your life, a life of fulfillment and joy, constantly creative and productive, one that always holds the possibility of surprise."

Hiring Our Heroes
(https://www.hiringourheroes.org/)
"Hiring Our Heroes (HOH) connects the military community—service members, military spouses, and veterans—with American businesses to create economic opportunity and a strong and diversified workforce."

Hire Heroes USA
(https://www.hireheroesusa.org/)
"Hire Heroes USA provides free job search assistance to U.S. military members, veterans and their spouses, and we help companies connect with opportunities to hire them."

Leading from Purpose
by Nick Craig
"If you don't know your purpose, you can't fully live it. If you aren't living it, you can't lead from it. *Leading From Purpose* will help you do both."

Sales Platoon
(https://www.mysalesplatoon.com/)
The bridge from military life, military skills and military discipline to civilian life requires a transition. A boot camp. An indoctrination. And that's exactly what we provide at Sales Platoon—with a focus on leveraging and translating highly skilled, resilient, dedicated, adaptive and disciplined men and women from active duty to a career that aligns well. A career in sales."

Signs of a Great Résumé
by Scott Vedder

"Scott's #1 best-selling book, *Signs of a Great Résumé*, will teach you how to write a résumé that speaks for itself. This lighthearted book presents an effective approach to the serious business of writing résumés. Scott's style is humorous, easy to understand, and fun to read ...if he does say so himself! Scott has developed a simple way to make your résumé speak for itself, using !@#$%, the Signs of a Great Résumé. Each sign showcases your experience and skills and highlights your greatest achievements and contributions."

Veterati
(https://www.veterati.com/)

"Join thousands of Service Members, Veterans, and Military Spouses in setting up free 1-hr. mentorship phone calls with successful professionals. We're the only Veteran Mentorship Platform to let you choose your own mentors and as many as you would like; our average member selects 4 mentors, and some mentees have 25+ mentors! Create a free profile at Veterati to get unlimited access to thousands of volunteer mentors: CEOs, recruiters, entrepreneurs, managers, veterans & civilians alike."